07-01

Best American Short Plays Series

THE
BEST
AMERICAN
SHORT
PLAYS
1998-1999

Edited with an Introduction by
GLENN YOUNG

APPLAUSE
NEW YORK • LONDON

An Applause Original

THE BEST AMERICAN SHORT PLAYS 1998-1999

Copyright ©2001 by Applause Theatre Book Publishers
All Rights Reserved
ISBN 1-55783-425-3 (cloth), 1-55783-429-6 (paper)
ISSN 0067-6284

Applause Theatre Book Publishers

151 West 46th Street
New York, NY 10023
Phone: (212) 575-9265
Fax: (646)-562-5852
Order Line: (800) 554-0626

Combined Book Service Ltd.

Units I/K,Paddock Wood
Distribution Centre
Paddock Wood, Tonbridge, Kent
TN126UU
Phone: (44) 01892 827171
Fax: (44) 01892 837272

First Applause Printing, 2001

For my old friend,
Joan Jurale

CONTENTS

INTRODUCTION

Absurdity and surrealism have acquired an odd verisimilitude. The new American Zeitgeist *is* made of sound bites. Time *has* lost its gravity. The writer of short plays no longer imposes brevity on Life so much as he hastily repackages it for audiences drunk on the rush of change and confusion. Reality itself really is short now — short-lived, with ever shorter attention spans, and painfully short on content. The current volatility of the stock market in any given day leaves behind the same graph that our parents watched accrue over months. Time magazine is written in sidebars, as History disintegrates into a hail of bullet points. The short plays in this volume may be more disturbing, and eerily more potent, than their forebears precisely because it is no longer our imaginations which recognize their disturbing premises but our own direct experience.

Theodore Apstein's plays first appeared in this series over half a century ago under the editorship of Margaret Mayorga. Apstein, in his other career as an educator, trained important writers and scholars, including Howard Stein, a distinguished man of the theatre and former co-editor of this series. Stein remains one of the formative influences in this editor's life and so the impromptu cycle trudges on. The appearance here of Apstein's final legacy, THE LIKENESS, following his death last year, closes the longest arc of any dramatist in this long-running series.

Apstein could not have known how aptly his play would foreshadow the knee-jerk intolerance of New York's mayor at a black female nude standing in for Jesus at the Brooklyn Museum. Four hundred years after Rembrandt used a young Jewish printer's apprentice as his model for Christ, we still prefer our Christs wearing Brooks Brothers suits.

The clear danger of censorship charges the air of Apstein's play. But the greater, more subversive danger addressed in the work may be the "purification" of the imagination. The persecution of both the "model" Jew and the fringe artist, Rembrandt, in Apstein's play warns us of most ruling cultures' pressure to recant any identity for which they have not issued state-sanctioned plates. It is, after all, how they remain in power, how they control us. Apstein captures the possibilities of life on the point of transcending those maddening restraints.

In attempting to do "justice" to his subject of Christ, where does Apstein's Rembrandt search for his model? In searching for truth, does the artist cling to his society's icons, or does he dare embrace the ambiguity of flesh and blood, fresh but unreliable? (This is the great gamble of the theatrical ritual itself. Will the artist invite unpredictable living collaborators to a table neatly set for communion? Can the people be trusted to take the sacrament? Will actors transubstantiate the text according to its stage directions?) Rembrandt's portrayal of Christ is based on a living Jew, not the church sanitized prototype. He is searching for the truth; they look for self-validation.

In Nathan, Apstein paints a young Jew trained by profession and tradition to make good, accurate printed copies. Like his model, Rembrandt, Nathan, chooses instead to stand out as an original human being — a model for the Renaissance's New Man. Apstein's notion of iconoclasm is not confined by museums or churches or artists. He offers us in the guise of 17th Century Amsterdam the original promise of the New World U.S.A., the high risk privilege of shattering, and possibly shedding, the idea we have inherited of ourselves.

Home may be the place where they have to take you in, but in Laura Cahill's HOME there's no room for the empty baggage of optimism Mary Jane brings with her. The American promise of regeneration hangs false and pathetic on the forty-year-old frame. Out for a "power walk" as the play opens, she's already assessing the assets of future husbands back in her New Jersey childhood home. But she ignores the unrecyclable lives of her dead father, the unredemptive lives of her self-exiled children, and the withered world of her childhood. Except for the final strains of the Good Humor man, her old hometown refuses her romantic call to resurrection. The home she was raised in is already scheduled to be sold to a neighbor who, unlike Mary Jane's mother Olivia, can afford the upkeep. Mary Jane has spent her life dodging consequences.

The mother's life has been hemmed in by them. The "cross-stitch" Olivia labors on throughout the play will not accommodate any false moves. Her careful budget will not allow another mouth to feed. The Great Depression carved its knife deep into Olivia, who remembers teetering on the brink of starvation as she held her mother's hand on the George Washington Bridge on their leap to meet Jesus. While Olivia's motive in revealing this horror story is to show her daughter how hard and unforgiving life really is, the result ironically is the uncovering of a certain rhythm of grace in the universe. Just as Olivia's mother was about to sweep them into eternity, a strange man stopped his car and gave Mother's mother the half dollar that bought their next meal. The revelation brings mother and daughter a step closer. Mary Jane has romanticized the past because she's never lived it. Her mother yearns for her own idyllic childhood in Tennessee, a state to which she longs to retire, because she hasn't allowed herself much freedom since. But before either of them can vacate the home where the action of the play takes place, each needs to check her psychic premises for ghosts, to test past deeds for spiritual encumbrances.

Television has so permeated American life that the medium has begun broadcasting on our nocturnal brainwaves. In Dave DeChristopher's FIFTEEN MINUTES, Nancy finally confronts her husband's infidelity on a tell-all cable talk show — produced on a heartstring budget — in their bedroom. Under the mega-wattage of the TV format, and tossing under the comic wraps of the play is a fundamental breakdown of the couple's communication. Under the titillating headline of "Infidelity: Stay Tuned," there lurks the terror of an impotence far greater than the sexual variety. (Can there be such a thing in America, where Viagra is now a bigger attraction than Niagara?) This couple seems incapable of consummating a single act of privacy. This is a different threat than Orwell's Big Brother, who invades your space and usurps it. It is different from The Truman Show, whose protagonist is unwittingly captured by the tube's glare. DeChristopher takes us into the new Survivor mode, where the private citizen gleefully surrenders his privacy to the all-seeing Cable Network. The couple's sexuality is replaced by the orgiastic cries of the audience. (DeChristopher supplants the mystery and majesty of the classic chorus with a single, simple-minded figure programmed to screech the most banal blood chants.) The ultimate intimacy has become a game show performed by these suburban gladiators in pj's, where every twist in the sheets is echoed down the long cable line by society's broadband indifference.

The Big Law Firm Interview is a sort of vestigial tribal experience of American Life. The Great Chief interviews the hopeful young warrior in a test of his agility, cunning and courage. American families make burnt sacrifices and whisper smoldering prayers that their offspring may be passed through to the Great White Shoe. Billy Goda in NO CRIME offers a fascinating dramatic assessment of how high the price such success can be, and how insidiously it may be extracted. Until now Cal has lived in an academic world of hypothetical murder and hypothetical blood. He's probably unbeatable in a virtual contest of legal skill. As Cal gracefully parries and thrusts his way through the ritual inquisition, we can only be impressed by the young litigator's preparation and ingenious resolve to win at all costs. What Cal is not prepared for is his first client. Goda has wrought a taut cautionary play about the slippery slope of the corporate ladder.

I DREAM BEFORE I TAKE THE STAND, Arlene Hutton's powerful woman's play, must make all of us shift positions in the night. A female rape victim is ostensibly being interviewed for the Facts. The male official conducting the interview probes and prods until, under his instruments of sweet sophistry, the fact-finding mission turns into not just one of those interrogations where the victim becomes the accused, but into a verbal reenactment of the crime. The source of the dramatic dynamic is purely Puritanical — Hutton's literary forebear is Hawthorne, not Freud. Any vital sign is read by the male official as an implied invitation to intercourse. Sentience in itself seems to imply nymphomania. The only fragrance a woman can safely wear in the park presumably is Raid. The only route across that park on a beautiful summer's day is along its perimeter. And thus are we banished from paradise.

Seven demi-monde playwrights in Tony Kushner's REVERSE TRANSCRIPTION break into a sacred New England cemetery where the likes of Lillian Hellman, Dashiell Hammett, John

Belushi and other luminaries are interred. The loquacious seven have convened from around the country to smuggle into this Yankee Westminster Abbey the body of their beloved departed friend and colleague, Ding; to dig, before dawn can discover their lunatic desecration, at long last and post mortem, their way into his unbeating heart. They commence to break bread together, indeed even to break wind together, and then to break (literary if not legal) convention together. But they cannot quite manage to break ground together. What is it that immobilizes these mortals from digging their friend's grave? Like the many final resting places in this symbolic graveyard, many are empty, cenotaphs of lives spent elsewhere. All seven are frozen by the nagging fear that when their own day of reckoning comes, there will be nobody buried under their tombstone. All are wondering if their names will be acknowledged by posterity, or will they for all eternity leave behind an unexhumed body of work? Deadlines encroach as dawn draws near.

Two men overhear the echoes from their own far-off lives in David Mamet's THE JADE MOUNTAIN. The action resonates between dream and myth, memory and factual outpost. The tea the men drink now tastes pallid compared to the musty exotic potion they conjure from the past.

John Ford Noonan is one of the great distinctive voices of his generation. While his career may not track the fashionable venues and broad boulevards of some of his more illustrious peers, one feels the superior potential in even his most modest efforts. In WHAT DROVE ME BACK TO RECONSIDERING MY FATHER, Noonan takes the clichéd trappings of the one-person play (e.g., telephone, tape machines, dolls) and makes each an essential part of his character's life. Dana is trapped not by the author's artifice — as in most solo drama — but by her own self-isolated condition. It is a measure of Noonan's genius that in his hands these worn out props become reanimated life supports, prosthetic limbs reaching out for human contact.

In Jules Tasca's DEUS-X, we are cascaded into an Aristophanic carnival of rare satiric energy in the American dramatic landscape. There is a savage undertow to Tasca's world that takes us deep into the realms of our schizophrenic social consciousness. Tasca's unbridled irreverence for pop religion and pseudo science runs to the edge of blasphemy, a line he does not hesitate to cross, or even double-cross. His characters come fully equipped with their own sound effects, flashbacks and laughtracks; they plunge into the present with choreographed ease and segue downstage to soliloquize outrageous asides. Tasca is one of the true originals of the form and a welcome repeat offender in this series.

We are entranced by the seductive strains of freedom in Tom Topor's BOUNTY COUNTY, IDAHO. His protagonist's cool ardor, the earnest logic of his patriotic argument envelop us in the banner of his cause. So hypnotic is his appeal that we are almost surprised by the growing repulsion inside us. Topor's anti-hero invites us to his homemade target range where we too can blow the heads off effigies of Jesse Jackson and Anita Hill. The casual reader might be forgiven for thinking this play a monologue. The other character doesn't speak for two reasons. First, the man she comes to interview isn't disposed, or even accustomed, to dialogue. His form of speech is related to his form of political expression: relentless barrage. He lays verbal siege to his interlocutor. Second, she's scared out of her wits. Literally dumbstruck. But the observant audience will hear her speak — louder even than the booming reports of her host's weaponry — in between the enemy lines.

In the bio she submitted for this volume, Cherie Vogelstein

explains she is "also an astro-physicist." That credential, although one suspects she meant "astral-physicist," is self-evident to anyone who knows her work. Vogelstein routinely speeds up the molecules of her plays. There is a sense of superheated premature déjà vu rocketing through all her work. Her comic timing is nothing less than cosmic. Like her 1993-94 Best American Short play DATE WITH A STRANGER, the characters in this latest short, ALL ABOUT AL, meet in a diner. Here we quickly relearn that the half-life of love for a Vogelstein character is measured in nanoseconds. Vogelstein's characters are not merely hungry for love. They are famished for it. They are bulemics of amour — gorging and then regurgitating in alternate bursts. Fast emotional food to the max. The editor looks forward to her next short play which he understands is entitled HEARTBURN.

Beckett and Genet never had to compete with CNN. The irony of television, and in particular of television "news," is that while it purports to be ultra-real, it has grown into the absolute opposite. Each passing year Television becomes an ever purer form of sensationalism. Producers like crack addicts strain to refine their drug down to the purest form. Beckett and Genet, like great playwrights in all eras, wrote disturbing things to jolt us to our senses. The modern media wishes to jolt us out of them, to better sell us soap. Theirs is pure drama without thought, without honor, and, aside from the commercial impulse, without purpose. The playwrights of this volume, with their few characters and homemade props, may struggle in this day and age to be heard over the din of our crazed New World, but in modest 99-seat houses, up flights of disrepair, they are still heard.

Glenn Young
New York City
November 2000

Theodore Apstein

THE LIKENESS

Theodore Apstein

Theodore Apstein's six one-act plays are published in *The Best Plays of the Year* and other anthologies and have been produced in the U.S. and abroad. His play *The Innkeepers* was done on Broadway, starring Geraldine Page and Darren McGavin, directed by Jose Quintero. *Come Share My House*, with Elisa Loti, was done off-Broadway and published by Samuel French. *Illusion* had a production at the New Dramatists Workshop and had a successful run in Spanish in Mexico City. *Sleight of Hand* was seen at UCLA, directed by Michael Gordon. *Manana is Another Day*, written in collaboration with Dwight Morris, was done at the Pasadena Playhouse, was published by Samuel French and has had numerous amateur productions.

Mr. Apstein's screenplays are *Whatever Happened to Aunt Alice?*, produced by Robert Aldrich and with a cast headed by Geraldine Page, Ruth Gordon, and Mildred Dunnock. *Baffled* starred Leonard Nimoy, Susan Hampshire and Rachel Roberts. *The Link* starred Michael Moriarty, Penelope Mildord and Geraldine Fitzgerald.

He has done many adaptations for television's Hallmark Hall of Fame (including Shaw's *Captain Brassbound's Conversion*, Anouilh's *Time Remembered*, *Johnny Belinda*) as well as original scripts for such series as *Studio One, Alcoa Playhouse, US Steel-Theatre Guild Hour, Danger, Suspense, Ben Casey, The Eleventh Hour, The Best Years, Dr. Kildare, Chrysler Theatre, Marcus Welby, The Waltons, Kung Fu*, etc. He has also functioned as a story editor on several television series.

He has taught playwriting at Columbia University and the American Theatre Wing and taught a graduate playwriting seminar at UCLA for almost 30 years. He founded and ran a playwrights' workshop at the Lee Strasberg Creative Center, was a member of the playwriting unit at the M.T. Forum and was active on committees in the Writers Guild of America West; he served as a member of its Board of Directors from 1978 to 1982.

CHARACTERS:
Nathan, grandson of Sarah
Sarah, Nathan's mother
Borch, older gentleman; stern and dignified

SETTING: *An all-purpose room in* SARAH's *house in Amsterdam. Seventeenth century. Night.*

SARAH *is asleep in a comfortable old armchair. The front door opens and her grandson* NATHAN *stumbles in. His clothes are torn and his face bloodied. He starts to take his coat off — it's painful because his arm hurts badly. He makes his way to the sideboard, pours water from the pitcher into a bowl and starts washing his face when* SARAH *wakes up.*

SARAH: Nathan. I thought you were still at the printshop. [*She rubs her eyes and takes a good look at him.*] Nathan! What happened to you? There's blood on your face — on your shirt — You've been fighting!

NATHAN: Two men jumped on me — on my way home. Maybe there were three.

SARAH: Oh, your poor nose —

NATHAN: Be careful, Bubbe, don't touch it. [*He touches it gingerly himself.*] I don't think it's broken.

SARAH: I hope not. Did they rob you?

NATHAN: No, they didn't do that.

SARAH: Let me clean up your face. [*She does with a cloth.*] Where does it hurt?

NATHAN: My chin ... my knee ... my arm. It's not too bad.

SARAH: Do you know who they were?

NATHAN: It was too dark to see any faces —

SARAH: Did they say anything?

NATHAN: They told me I'm a goddamn Jew. As if I didn't know.

SARAH: All the years we've lived in Amsterdam this never happened to us.

NATHAN: You've never been called a goddamn Jew?

SARAH: Oh, yes, but I've never been beaten up.

NATHAN: They're furious at me.

SARAH: Who? You said you don't know who those men were.

NATHAN: I don't, but there are other people who —

SARAH: I don't understand what you're saying. Did you do something wrong?

NATHAN: No, I didn't.

SARAH: I'll heat up some milk for you.

NATHAN: Later, Bubbe. I have to go out now.

SARAH: Where? I'm not letting you go out again tonight.

NATHAN: I have to.

SARAH: It's too dangerous. [*She continues cleaning his face.*]

NATHAN: There's somebody I have to warn. They might hurt him too.

SARAH: Nathan, what's going on? You said they're furious at you. Who?

NATHAN: Everybody who's seen the painting. And everybody who's heard about it.

SARAH: What painting?

NATHAN: I sat for a painting —

SARAH: What! When did you do that? You've always told me everything ...

NATHAN: I didn't tell you because I knew you'd ask a thousand questions.

SARAH: I'm asking them now! Why would you sit for a painting? You're a printer, you're a serious, hard-working young man. Did they pay you a lot of money?

NATHAN: It was not for pay. That's not why I did it. I was just very flattered when Rembrandt asked me to sit for him.

SARAH: Rembrandt? The one that lives in the big house on the edge of the Jewish district?

[*And as* NATHAN *nods, she adds.*]

A big house, but no money. Your grandfather always let him have
herring on account. I heard he painted pictures. Are they at least
pretty pictures?

NATHAN: They're more than pretty. Rich people ask him to do their
portraits and this year he sold a picture to a nobleman who lives
a long way from Amsterdam — in Italy.

SARAH: If your Rembrandt is so good, why is there all this ado over
the picture?

NATHAN: Some people don't agree with the way he paints. They
don't like …

SARAH: Your picture?

NATHAN: They don't like what it shows …

SARAH: Nathan! Did he paint you in the nude? I know painters do
that, but my grandson will not pose naked. I will die of shame!

NATHAN: I'm fully dressed. In a costume of the period.

SARAH: What period?

NATHAN: Biblical.

SARAH: You represent somebody in the Bible? What can be bad
about that?

NATHAN: It's the way people look at it …

[*Reaches for his coat and gets into it.*]

SARAH: If you're wearing a costume, it can't be Adam. Moses? You don't look like Moses. I don't know why we always think of him as an old man, but we do.

NATHAN: No, I didn't portray Moses.

SARAH: A prophet? Elijah? [*And before* NATHAN *can reply.*] Is Rembrandt going to sell the picture?

NATHAN: I hope he does — he always seems to be short of money.

SARAH: He didn't choose a good trade.

NATHAN: But I think he enjoys his work. He made me enjoy it too — because I wasn't just posing — he made me feel I was really a part of what he was doing.

SARAH: There — your face is clean.

NATHAN: Thank you, Bubbe — you're always so good to me.

SARAH: I'm just repaying in kind. I know taking care of an old woman is no fun for a young man.

NATHAN: But you're the one who takes care of me.

SARAH: [*Rolling up* NATHAN's *sleeve.*] I'm going to look at your arm ...

NATHAN: It's not bleeding. I have to go, Bubbe.

[NATHAN *buttons his jacket and goes to the door.* SARAH *stops him.*]

SARAH: What if they attack you again? Please don't go out.

NATHAN: I have to tell Rembrandt.

SARAH: It's him you're worried about? They won't attack him — he's not a Jew. Don't get mixed up in anything, Nathan — you don't need that. You have a good chance of becoming a master printer — like your father dreamed you would be — even if he didn't live to see it.

NATHAN: I may have lost that chance — with so many people turning against me.

SARAH: Because of that painting? Well, we'll do something about it. I know what. That Rembrandt ate our fish for free — the time has come for him to pay back. Tell him to hand that painting over to you.

NATHAN: How can I ask him to do that?

SARAH: With words! If you don't, I will. If the picture makes trouble, it's best to get it out of sight.

NATHAN: When he paints a picture, the world has to see it.

SARAH: The world will be deprived this time. The picture will be in our possession. In mine. Better still, we'll burn it.

NATHAN: No! It's wrong to burn something like that.

SARAH: So I'll hide it.

NATHAN: I told you it should be seen — it must be seen. I'm going to his house.

SARAH: Wait —

[NATHAN *starts to leave, but a knock at the door stops him.* SARAH *is alarmed and hesitantly moves toward the door. There is another knock.* NATHAN *holds her back, takes over and opens the door. He is faced by* BORCH, *a stern, dignified man, who is coming in from outside.*]

BORCH: Forgive me for such a late visit.

SARAH: [*Bowing.*] Mynheer Borch.

BORCH: You don't have to bow to me. [*To* NATHAN.] Are you Nathan the printer?

NATHAN: The printer's helper.

SARAH: He's very modest, my grandson. He started as an apprentice, but nowadays he's second only to the master printer himself. Please have a seat, Mynheer.

BORCH: Thank you. I do not customarily stay up this late and certainly don't make calls, but we felt this was something that should be taken care of at once.

NATHAN: I've heard this "*we*" all day long, and I still don't know who it is.

BORCH: Perhaps it is all of Amsterdam. It is certainly the elders of my church, which you may know has the largest congregation in this city. We had a very long meeting tonight and I was delegated to speak to you, Nathan. But you were about to go out, I believe?

SARAH: He doesn't have to.

NATHAN: Yes, I do. I have to talk to someone …

BORCH: Rembrandt perhaps? You can't talk to him now because one of my brethren is paying him a visit at this very moment.

SARAH: Are they beating him up too?

BORCH: What?

SARAH: Look at what they did to my grandson.

BORCH: That's too bad. I am sure it wasn't anyone from my congregation. Certainly not one of the elders.

NATHAN: No, they just ignite the fire.

SARAH: Don't be disrespectful, Nathan.

NATHAN: Why are they so irritated by the painting?

BORCH: You've seen it, have you?

NATHAN: Of course I have.

BORCH: [To SARAH.] Have you?

SARAH: No. I didn't even know that Nathan had posed —

BORCH: I haven't seen the painting myself, but the nephew of one of our elders happened to be in Rembrandt's house earlier today and saw the canvas. He found it quite intolerable.

NATHAN: Why intolerable?

SARAH: Don't interrupt him, Nathan.

BORCH: What was intolerable was to see your face in a painting entitled "Christ at Emmaus." I understand there are several figures in the picture, but your likeness is unmistakable on the one that purports to be Jesus.

NATHAN: Yes, that's the one I sat for.

SARAH: You — sat — for Jesus?

BORCH: So you knew!

NATHAN: Of course Rembrandt told me what the painting was about.

BORCH: I'd forgotten the name of the place was Emmaus.

NATHAN: There were two or three villages with the same name, but it's probably the one that's closest to Jerusalem.

SARAH: How do you know all that? [To BORCH.] He always thinks he's so smart. [Back to NATHAN.] But you're not smart at all. You're stupid to sit for such a picture. No wonder the elders are furious. I'm furious myself. Why did you do it?

NATHAN: I like Rembrandt. Every time I'm in his house I learn something. That's how I found out about Emmaus. And about so many things from the Bible.

SARAH: You never showed much interest in the Bible before. What happened in this place called Emmaus?

NATHAN: It's where Jesus appeared three days after the crucifixion.

SARAH: He couldn't have appeared — he was dead.

BORCH: How dare you say that? He was there because he was resurrected.

SARAH: As you well know, Mynheer, we Jews don't believe in that.

NATHAN: Not literally, Bubbe, but if you take it symbolically ...

SARAH: Symbolically! Now, there's a word for you. You never used to talk this way. But you're not going to confuse me. I know nobody has ever been resurrected.

BORCH: Except in this one instance.

NATHAN: Please, Mynheer, you would do well not to get into a debate about religion with my grandmother.

BORCH: I have no intention of doing that. But the elders are not willing to accept the face of a Jew as that of Jesus.

NATHAN: However, Jesus was ...

BORCH: [*Breaks in.*] Don't get scholarly with me.

NATHAN: He was unquestionably a Jew until all the nonsense began about calling him the son of God.

BORCH: Now you're being irreverent. Why did Rembrandt choose you to be Jesus?

NATHAN: He said my face spoke to him.

BORCH: Don't get it into your head that you are divine.

SARAH: My grandson is a sensible young man!

BORCH: Perhaps he used to be sensible. But a few days ago he tried to walk on the Amstel River.

SARAH: He didn't!

BORCH: Several of my brethren saw him.

SARAH: Nathan!

NATHAN: One of my friends dared me.

SARAH: To walk on the Amstel?

NATHAN: He said if you're Jesus in Rembrandt's painting, why not on the water?

SARAH: It's a miracle you didn't drown. Miracle ... what am I saying?

NATHAN: It wasn't a miracle, Bubbe. My friend stopped me. But isn't it wonderful what a man can do if he believes.

SARAH: Believes what?

NATHAN: Anything.

SARAH: Has Rembrandt been trying to convert you? I don't know what's come over you.

BORCH: Tell your grandmother about the merchants.

NATHAN: What for? It didn't do any good.

BORCH: He said he would run the moneychangers out of the temple. Reminds you of someone, doesn't it?

SARAH: How could you do such a thing, Nathan?

NATHAN: I didn't say I'd run them out — I was just talking to two of the merchants and — I told them it wouldn't hurt them to be more honest.

SARAH: What business is it of yours?

BORCH: You are not Jesus!

SARAH: Don't you see, Mynheer? Rembrandt has filled his ears with bad thoughts.

NATHAN: It's not a bad thought to try to make the world better.

SARAH: Leave that to the Rabbi. You're a printer's helper.

BORCH: Improving the world is a very large undertaking. We have learned men to deal with that.

NATHAN: But they often forget to do it. The elders of your church are presumed to be wise men, but what are they busy with? Judging me. Why am I their concern?

SARAH: [To BORCH.] He'll never sit for that painter again.

NATHAN: Don't promise that. Rembrandt said he may need me for another picture.

SARAH: But you won't do it!

NATHAN: I will if he asks me. He's tired of all the portraits of Jesus looking like a Nordic saint. Why did they always paint him with flowing blond hair and blue eyes?

SARAH: Because that's the way they want him to look! But no, it's not good enough for Rembrandt!

NATHAN: Jesus lived in Palestine — it's a reasonable guess that he didn't look Nordic.

BORCH: But it doesn't prove he looked Jewish. No one recorded his face during his lifetime. The ones who painted him later had to rely on their imaginations. Which could've easily led them to sinful mistakes.

NATHAN: What mistakes? We can't even be certain that Jesus existed.

BORCH: Yes, we can!

SARAH: Indeed we can!

NATHAN: You too?

SARAH: We know that a man who caused a great deal of trouble in Judea was put to death.

BORCH: [*Looking sternly at* NATHAN.] Crucified.

NATHAN: Are you trying to frighten me, Mynheer?

BORCH: [*Looks angrily at* NATHAN, *then turns to* SARAH.] You would be wise to speak to Rembrandt and express your distaste for that painting.

SARAH: Oh, I will, but Nathan says Rembrandt won't destroy it.

BORCH: Perhaps there can be a less drastic remedy. Perhaps you could persuade him to use a different model for the face of Jesus.

NATHAN: No ... He'll never agree to do that.

SARAH: He can't erase your face and replace it with another? What kind of a painter is he?

NATHAN: I don't want him to change what he did. When he was painting, it was the first time I had a little understanding of what it means to help make something that never existed before — the wonder of something happening before your eyes — it must be not unlike what God did when there was nothing.

BORCH: Be careful — you're blaspheming.

SARAH: Do you want the Rabbi to throw you out of our congregation?

BORCH: I was under the impression that it's forbidden for you Jews to represent the Deity in pictures.

NATHAN: Very true, but Jesus is not a deity for us.

BORCH: You don't have to be clever with me. He's a deity for Rembrandt.

SARAH: I don't want people to see it! We don't need a Jew posing as a Christian.

BORCH: We don't need it either. [To NATHAN.] You could succeed in turning the entire Christian population of Amsterdam against your people.

NATHAN: My people aren't responsible ...

SARAH: But we're always blamed. [*To* BORCH, *apologetically.*] Nathan sat for that painting just as a favor for Rembrandt. [*To* NATHAN.] What he painted didn't matter to you, did it?

NATHAN: I had no idea how much it mattered. But now I want my face — my Jewish face — to be there and for everybody to see it.

BORCH: If you defy your community, you will end up badly.

NATHAN: If I don't, Mynheer, I will end up worse. I wouldn't be myself anymore.

SARAH: What's happening to you, Nathan?

NATHAN: To me? I've been pounded by ruffians and threatened by an elder. I don't like the way they're treating me.

SARAH: But you provoked them, you and Rembrandt.

NATHAN: I don't like the way you're treating me either. I always thought my own grandmother would respect me as I've respected her. [*He goes to the door.*] You're in my way, Mynheer. I'm going to see Rembrandt. [*He leaves.*]

BORCH: He's stubborn and rebellious.

SARAH: Yes, he is. But isn't he strong?

BORCH: You sound proud of him.

SARAH: Do I? Then I suppose I am, Mynheer. I'd like to see that painting. I wonder if Rembrandt did justice to my Nathan.

CURTAIN

Laura Cahill

HOME

Laura Cahill

Laura Cahill is the author of the full-length plays *Hysterical Blindness* (soon to be an HBO film starring Uma Thurman) and *Mercy*, and the one-acts *Home* and *Jersey Girls Go to the Park*. *Hysterical Blindness*, *Mercy* and *Home* are all published by Dramatists Play Service. *Home* can also be found in the anthology *Marathon 1996* published by Smith and Kraus. Her plays have been produced or workshopped at the Vineyard Theater, New Harmony Project, PS NBC, Naked Angels and EST's Marathon '96. She wrote a pilot script for the WB network and has written for episodic television. She begins work soon on a three-script deal with Miramax Films.

CHARACTERS:
Olivia, mother of Mary Jane, 60's.
Mary Jane, daughter of Olivia, 40's

SETTING: *The living room of a small development house in New Jersey. It is just after twilight on a Saturday in early summer.*

The furniture is Colonial reproductions and nothing is expensive. The room is kept immaculately clean.

OLIVIA, *60's, sits on the couch with her cross stitch.* MARY JANE, *40's and very youthful, walks in the front door. She is dressed in worn tight blue jeans and a cheap-looking top. She wears sneakers. This is her exercise ensemble. Her Walkman is on and she sings along loudly with the oldie she's listening to as she stretches out from her speed-walk.*

MARY JANE: [*Heading to the kitchen.*] I saw two men that I could tell weren't married. One was walking a dog which I think is pretty good. Men with dogs are more open and friendly, you know?

OLIVIA: Your father always had a dog, from the day I met him he had a dog. I bought Coke. You must be thirsty from all that running.

[MARY JANE *emerges from the kitchen with a can of Coke.*]

MARY JANE: One fellow looked about 40 to 45. Which is a good age. The other one was a little older, 50 to 52. [*She walks in and sits with her mother.*] And he was walking just for exercise, which is real good, real good, Ma, right? A man who walks for exercise isn't afraid of living. Isn't that right?

OLIVIA: Maybe he's recovering from a bypass.

MARY JANE: I don't know about that.

OLIVIA: They tell you to go out and walk every day after a bypass. That's what Daddy would've been doing right now.

MARY JANE: And Daddy loved living, see? See what I mean? I think I did good.

OLIVIA: But you didn't talk to them?

MARY JANE: No, not on the first day. I gotta let them notice me for a while. Divorcee back in town, free as a bird, loves to laugh and take long drives.

OLIVIA: Good. There's no big hurry. You could meet a husband anywhere, really.

MARY JANE: I wanna meet him here. [*Pause.* MARY JANE *waits for a response.* OLIVIA *doesn't look up.*] You know what I did on my way back? I walked down by the railroad tracks.

OLIVIA: Nobody walks down there anymore.

MARY JANE: I used to practically every day. There used to be that candy store, remember? Me and Susie'd sit on the curb in front drinking a Coke. There were those boys who'd come by. Bobby Panko and Tommy Hansen and Billy Marsh. They'd drive up in their cars ... one by one ... "You wanna go for a ride, Mary Jane?" God, that was a lifetime ago. I wonder if anyone else remembers that but me.

OLIVIA: People don't think about things like that.

MARY JANE: I don't know. They might.

OLIVIA: People learn to move on.

MARY JANE: What? Are you picking on me already? I didn't come three thousand miles to get picked on.

OLIVIA: Oh, sorry. I didn't realize I was picking on anybody. I thought I was just sitting in my living room minding my own business.

MARY JANE: You think you'd be a little happier to hear me talk like this. Here I am coming home after all this time and looking for a nice husband.

OLIVIA: You think you'd be a little more concerned with someone else once in a while —

MARY JANE: I am.

OLIVIA: Like your mother.

MARY JANE: I am concerned.

OLIVIA: I have a lot on my mind today.

MARY JANE: I'm concerned with what's on your mind.

[*Pause.* OLIVIA *waits for* MARY JANE. *She doesn't respond.*]

OLIVIA: Coulda fooled me.

MARY JANE: When I get a husband maybe we'll have the wedding right here in this room. I think that's what this house needs now. Huh, Ma?

OLIVIA: We'll have to see.

MARY JANE: It'll be great. Everything's gonna work out for me. You'll see. Okay?

OLIVIA: Okay.

MARY JANE: I walked past the St. Cecelia's fairgrounds, you know. Remember how the men would pay to fight with a live bear on that little stage the Monsignor put up every year? I'm sure they don't do that anymore.

OLIVIA: No.

MARY JANE: That would be considered old-fashioned to people now. It's so funny 'cause I used to think when I was a kid the world had already changed just in time for my childhood — and that everything was modern. But actually it was real old-fashioned when I was a kid. That stuff we all thought about the world then wasn't true at all. And then the world did change and it was without me even noticing it … and it didn't have anything to do with me. My childhood was old-fashioned, Ma. It wasn't as golden and as special as we all thought. Isn't that funny?

OLIVIA: I suppose.

MARY JANE: I was walking past the fairgrounds and I could picture where everything would be and the crowds of people that would come and I could almost smell the sausage the ladies'd make. And you know, it may be changed a lot, but it's not all gone. There's so much here I can rediscover, even. I was realizing that today and I was so happy, Ma, 'cause I was thinking that this year I'm gonna be here for the fair. It's only a month away. A month from tomorrow exactly.

OLIVIA: Is it?

MARY JANE: And maybe I'll take Daddy's place and I'll work in the beer tent this year. And you can visit me every night. I bet I can meet men that way, huh?

OLIVIA: Maybe. We'll see.

MARY JANE: How many years do you think Daddy worked the fair?

OLIVIA: Well, a lot.

MARY JANE: Probably forty.

OLIVIA: Oh, I'm sure.

MARY JANE: Wow. [*Pause.*] Wow. [*Pause.*] It's so quiet here tonight, isn't it?

OLIVIA: It's been like that. Sometimes I lose track of the time of day and I end up walking around this house alone at three in the morning. I get the times all mixed up.

MARY JANE: Well, that's one reason it's good to have me home.

OLIVIA: Mm-hmm.

MARY JANE: I'm glad I'm here, anyway.

OLIVIA: There's no reason for you to be in California anymore.

MARY JANE: It's more than that. This was the best thing for me to do. It was really the best, you know? I'm glad you asked me to come back.

OLIVIA: Well, you wanted to. It was your idea.

MARY JANE: I think you asked.

OLIVIA: Okay, I'm wrong I suppose.

MARY JANE: Never mind. I'm here. That's all that matters. But I'm planning on getting out and finding a job soon.

OLIVIA: Things are so expensive here.

MARY JANE: I know that, Ma. I'm gonna get a nice job. Maybe in that new office park across from the Mall.

OLIVIA: Well, you could work anywhere.

MARY JANE: I know.

OLIVIA: That's the great thing about being young. You can just pick up and go.

MARY JANE: What are you saying?

OLIVIA: Nothing.

MARY JANE: You're saying something.

OLIVIA: No. [*Pause.*] The other night I was in the Shop-Rite and I ran into Mrs. Harris and her youngest girl. She's getting married and they're looking for their first house.

MARY JANE: Yeah?

OLIVIA: They've been looking and looking all over town. So I said you should come look at mine, I have exactly what you're trying to find.

MARY JANE: What?

OLIVIA: She was so thrilled. She took my hands and said, "Mrs. Dunn, I always loved your house from the outside when I used to pass it every day on my way to school."

MARY JANE: It's a development. They all look exactly the same.

OLIVIA: She said there was always something special about it. She remembered the white candles I'd put in the window at Christmas and the plastic life-size witch I'd hang on the front door at Halloween to scare all the kids. She said, "Mrs. Dunn. It's a dream come true for me to have your house. I wouldn't do a thing to it." I was so flattered.

MARY JANE: What?

OLIVIA: So they're coming to take a look around.

MARY JANE: Mother.

OLIVIA: Well, I never said I was happy here.

MARY JANE: You didn't say anything.

OLIVIA: Then you should've asked me.

MARY JANE: But I didn't know there was anything wrong.

OLIVIA: How could you not know? How could you think I could stay here? That's just silly. You're just being silly now. Of course I can't stay here.

MARY JANE: I just can't believe this. There's no reason for this.

OLIVIA: No reason? Tell my friends that. Call them up and tell them there's no reason to leave and that they should all come back. That it doesn't cost too much to heat a house here and the taxes aren't too high here, that we're not too old and our husbands aren't really gone now and we can all sit on the back porch and eat potato salad and hamburgers again and not know when it's all going to end.

MARY JANE: It didn't end. Don't say that. I know things are different now. I can see that. I'm not blind. But we have to stay right here, Ma.

OLIVIA: Okay. What are you gonna do when we starve, then? Throw me away?

MARY JANE: What? Mother!

OLIVIA: Life is too hard here.

MARY JANE: It's hard everywhere. It's harder out there. Where do you even think we're gonna go? I don't know where on earth you think we're gonna go.

OLIVIA: I don't know.

MARY JANE: You don't know. Great. Well, you should think of someplace to go. You can't sell this house without some idea of where you plan on ending up. Even I know that.

OLIVIA: Tennessee.

MARY JANE: So you decided. Why do you always keep secrets? You always just sit with your mouth closed and nobody ever knows what you're thinking.

OLIVIA: I don't have to tell you everything.

MARY JANE: You were always like this. Always like this. I was 19 years old and you coulda stopped me from going to California with Jimbo to begin with and my life woulda —

OLIVIA: Nobody coulda stopped you.

MARY JANE: You didn't even try! I was your daughter and you didn't care where I ended up.

OLIVIA: That's ridiculous. You didn't care where you ended up.

MARY JANE: Oh right, of course, you're Miss Innocent again, Ma.

OLIVIA: Oh, I'm Miss Innocent? You make one mistake after another for 20 years and you never took responsibility for one second! You brought babies into this world that you could barely feed 'cause that husband a yours couldn't hold down a job.

MARY JANE: That's such a lie! How could you say that?

OLIVIA: [Overlapping.] Oh, keep your voice down.

MARY JANE: [Overlapping.] He got laid off that time, Ma! Laid off!

[OLIVIA jumps up and shuts the windows.]

OLIVIA: [Overlapping.] You don't have to broadcast it to the world.

MARY JANE: [Overlapping.] And we woulda paid back every penny of that money but Daddy said it was okay not to. Okay not to! You hear me, Ma?

OLIVIA: [Overlapping.] The whole neighborhood can hear you!

MARY JANE: [Overlapping.] So don't you ever bring that up again!

OLIVIA: [Overlapping.] You should be ashamed of that fresh mouth of yours.

MARY JANE: That's all you care about, isn't it? What the neighbors think and where the neighbors are moving to. This is my second chance. I don't know where I'm gonna go now. You're turning my life upside down.

OLIVIA: You don't have any idea what it means to have your life turned upside down.

MARY JANE: That's ridiculous. That's so utterly ridiculous.

OLIVIA: I can't believe you're doing this to me.

MARY JANE: I can't believe you're doing this to me. I guess my plans don't matter. Do they? The failure daughter comes home but that's just not good enough for you, I guess.

OLIVIA: Just shut up. Shut up.

MARY JANE: You shut up. You just shut up forever. How about that? [*She rushes into the bedroom.*] I'm so sick of this.

[*She returns with a suitcase, throws it on the floor. She goes back again and retrieves some clothes and things. She throws them on top of the suitcase.*]

OLIVIA: What are you doing?

MARY JANE: What's it matter? It so obviously doesn't matter to you. [*She packs.*]

OLIVIA: Okay. Okay. You do what you have to do. I'm not gonna keep you here. Leave your mother to do everything herself. Just go ahead and go.

MARY KAY: I am.

OLIVIA: Where do you think you're gonna go?

MARY JANE: I don't know.

[OLIVIA'*s up and trying to stop* MARY JANE.]

OLIVIA: Just stop it. [*They fight over the suitcase.*] Stop it now!

MARY JANE: No!

OLIVIA: Stop! Let go. Be a big girl now.

MARY JANE: Give me my stuff!

OLIVIA: Come on. Let go!

MARY JANE: Ma!! [*She gives up and throws the clothes down. She jumps up and walks away.* OLIVIA *quickly unpacks all the clothes and closes the suitcase.*] I guess I should have stayed in Bakersfield.

OLIVIA: No, Mary Jane.

MARY JANE: Oh yeah? At least I didn't have any dreams to get broken again while I was there. At least I knew I didn't deserve any. I was fine before you called me and told me I did. Why'd I believe you? Huh? Why?

OLIVIA: I meant what I said on the phone. That you should start again. I meant that.

MARY JANE: I thought this time you were gonna help me.

OLIVIA: I can't help you.

MARY JANE: But Ma. I can't go back to California. I don't have any money to go anywhere. As soon as you called me and ASKED me to come here I started thinking about all kinds of things and it started looking up again. Coming back kind of washed away all my mistakes. I can't explain it but it did. It did.

OLIVIA: Don't be silly.

MARY JANE: I'm not being silly.

OLIVIA: Well you're not making any sense. I hope you don't go around talking to people like this.

MARY KAY: I don't.

OLIVER: You're young and strong. That's all that matters.

MARY KAY: I'm not that young.

OLIVIA: You can do whatever you want. You don't have the worries that I have in my head morning, noon and night.

MARY JANE: What worries?

OLIVIA: Oh, I don't know. I don't know.

[OLIVIA *sits on the couch. And picks up her cross stitch. Her hands shake and she can't concentrate but she pretends. She cries.*]

MARY JANE: [*Impatiently.*] Don't cry, Ma.

OLIVIA: I'm not crying. I have never cried in front of my child.

[*They sit in silence.*]

MARY JANE: I like being back here, you know. And it's good to be around all the memories of Daddy. And when my boys come and visit there's room for them, you know? Zachary will get leave from the army and maybe he'll come and visit. And Nathaniel might start making good money in Wyoming and wanna come to New Jersey and see us. Maybe with that new girlfriend. Please, Ma. Things are gonna be easier now, for both of us.

OLIVIA: Nobody said things were supposed to be easy. [Beat.] My poor mother ... she had it so hard.

MARY JANE: Grandma did? How?

OLIVIA: Well there was a Depression, Mary Jane, don't you know anything?

MARY JANE: Yes I know there was a Depression, but how did I know it affected Grandma?

OLIVIA: It affected everybody. Is that what I sent you to school for? They didn't teach you anything.

MARY JANE: Well, excuse me.

OLIVIA: Your Grandmother had her cross to bear with two little girls and no food and my father dead. We were starving. All three of us. The landlady put us out. She woke us up real early one Sunday morning and put us out on the streets of New York City.

MARY JANE: What?

OLIVIA: So I said, "What are we gonna do, Mother?" And she said, "First we go to Mass. It is Sunday." I was afraid I was going to go to Hell 'cause I knelt down and blessed myself while at the same time I was thinking what are we doing here, this can't help us.

MARY JANE: This really happened?

OLIVIA: My mother asked at the rectory for food and blankets to sleep in the park but they shut the door right on us. I thought God was punishing me, maybe he was. We slept in Central Park that night with nothing. And the whole time I'm waiting for my trip to hell 'cause I was sure it was coming. My mother and me and Aunt Carol walked the streets all day and we weren't talking. And finally my mother took us up on the George Washington Bridge. The three of us were sitting up on the bridge all afternoon and I had no idea why. And finally my mother said, "See the water? If you hold on to Mother as tight as you can we can all go into the water and we'll be together forever with Jesus."

MARY JANE: Ma.

OLIVIA: And Carol started to cry. Mother said, "Jesus loves us. Jesus loves us. You will never be hungry again." We were starving to death and I knew it. So we all held on real tight together and walked to the edge of the bridge, but I let go. 'Cause I knew I wouldn't get to heaven with them. And Grandma couldn't jump off that bridge without both her girls. By then a man in a car stopped and he gave my mother a half dollar to feed us.

MARY JANE: He saved your life.

OLIVIA: Well it worked out fine, Mary Jane. We went to a luncheonette on the New Jersey side. And she called her first cousin who had married a man from the south and moved to Tennessee. Her cousin had no money but they said, "We have a farm and can feed ourselves. So if you send your girls we can feed them too." So me and my sister went on a train to live with strangers. I thought it was heaven. Green and blue everywhere I looked, and we could pick crab apples and sink our teeth right in them. [*Beat.*] We didn't see our mother for eight years. It was very hard. As soon as I got back up here and lived with Grandma in New Jersey, I met Daddy and went off and got married. Carol stayed with Grandma, though, for a few years.

MARY JANE: I can't believe this story. Why didn't you ever tell me?

OLIVIA: It's not the kind of thing you go around telling people about.

MARY JANE: Telling people? I'm your daughter.

OLIVIA: Well, whatever, Mary Jane.

MARY JANE: You told me now. Today. Why'd you tell me now?

OLIVIA: It came up.

MARY JANE: You wanted me to know. You told me 'cause you wanted me to know.

[*Pause.* MARY JANE *sits and thinks.* OLIVIA *suddenly opens up.*].

OLIVIA: You know, I was scared of the ocean my whole life. But when you were four and we took you down the shore you took one look at the water and said, "Mommy, I'm gonna have to go out there." And I said, "Oh no, Mary Jane, those waves are gonna knock you down." And you said, "I know they will but I'll get right back up again and swim hard." And that's just what you did.

MARY JANE: Really? [*Pause.*] You know why I left? You're not gonna believe it when I tell you. I really wanted to live in a van. A light blue Chevy van with white trim. But Jimbo didn't listen to me, he got a black van. But, I figured — it's still a van. It was the only thing I really wanted. Can you believe that my only goal was to live in a van? You said to me when I was leaving, "What is going on in your head?" And I made up all this stuff, but that was it. That was all I was thinking.

OLIVIA: How on earth did you come up with an idea like that one? You can't shower or go to the bathroom or cook a meal on a van.

MARY JANE: Well, that's true. [*Beat.*] It's good to talk like this.

OLIVIA: People talk too much these days. They think it solves the world's problems.

MARY JANE: But you can tell people what you want. You can tell me, you know, what's going on in your head?

OLIVIA: I want to go home. I can't do it alone. When Daddy died you said you were coming. Back to New Jersey. I thought oh, now I have someone again. Someone to take me home.

MARY JANE: Oh, Ma.

OLIVIA: I'm sorry.

MARY JANE: No. Don't say you're sorry. I don't want you to ever say you're sorry to me. [*She sits near her mother.*] It's okay, Ma. It's okay. [*She takes* OLIVIA's *cross stitch into her hands.*] Oh, this is so nice.

OLIVIA: It's a house. I bought it in the crafts store but I changed the colors of the thread myself, to green and white. To stand for our house.

MARY JANE: Yeah. It's really beautiful.

OLIVIA: Well I try.

[*An ice cream truck rings its bell.*]

MARY JANE: An ice cream truck? [*She gets up and goes to the front door and opens it.*] There's still an ice cream truck?

OLIVIA: Why don't you go get some? Go ahead, stop him.

MARY JANE: Okay. I think I will. [*She stops and turns back toward her mother.*] Ma, remember the song we'd sing? [*Sing-song.*] "SAM! SAM! The Good Humor man!" All the kids would sing for Sam to stop.

OLIVIA: And your father! He loved to sing that song too. You could hear him all the way up the street.

MARY JANE: Are you kidding, you could hear him a mile away.

[MARY JANE *has stopped, stares out the screen door.*]

OLIVIA: Well you better run!

MARY JANE: No. I don't wanna. I'd rather just remember it.

OLIVIA: Well. You won't get any ice cream that way.

[MARY JANE *stares out the door, memorizing her old neighborhood.*]

MARY JANE: That's okay. [*Pause.*] The best thing about any place is remembering it. [*Neighborhood sounds get louder.*] I like to remember everything exactly. [*Pause.*] Hear that lawn mower? I love that sound.

OLIVIA: Yeah, I suppose that's a nice sound. [*She thinks.*] Comforting. Isn't it?

MARY JANE: [*Still staring out.*] Yeah. It's comforting. [*She looks to her mother. Beat.*] We'll go to Tennessee. Me and you. And we'll be home. [*Looking out the door.*] We'll be home.

END OF PLAY

Dave DeChristopher

FIFTEEN MINUTES

Dave DeChristopher

Dave DeChristopher attended Washington and Lee University and Hunter College, where he studied playwriting with Tina Howe and Lavonne Mueller. His plays include *The Jack Report, Home Fires, Moon Vault, Brutes, Past Palpable* and *Hand-Me-Downs*. These (and other) works have been produced in San Francisco, Pittsburgh, Los Angeles, Milwaukee, Chicago, and in more than twenty New York City theatres. In the 1980s, Dave authored two long-running paperback book series. Currently, he is the artistic director of the Greenwood Theater Company (a theater-in-education company), a member of the Castillo Theatre acting ensemble, and a busy artist-in-the-schools. He is a founding member of the Aural Stage, a New York-based alliance of playwrights, actors, and directors. Dave is also one of the country's leading cruciverbalists. He led the 1996 playwriting workshop at the Sewanee Writers' Conference, along with Romulus Linney. He was a contributing writer to the Washington weekly, *The Hill*, from 1996-99.

CHARACTERS:
Nancy, our hostess
Anthony, her husband
Audience, a woman in pink
Libby, Nancy's guest
Dr. Allegra Shayne-Bledsoe

TIME: *One A.M. on a Tuesday*

PLACE: NANCY *and* ANTHONY'*s bedroom*

Lights come up to half. NANCY *is sitting up in bed next to* ANTHONY, *who is asleep. She has just turned on the lamp on her bedside table. She speaks to a downstage figure in a chair, fuzzily seen at this point.*

NANCY: Welcome to "*Nancy After Dark*". Tonight we're talking about infidelity — who does it, who they do it to, and what about the children? Stay tuned.

[*She strikes an animated pose, freezes for a few seconds. Downstage figure applauds.* NANCY *pushes a button on a tape recorder on bedside table near lamp. Innocuous theme music fills the stage, waking* ANTHONY.]

ANTHONY: What!?

[*He sits up groggily.*]

NANCY: [*Through a frozen smile.*] Shhh!

ANTHONY: What? What are you doing?

[ANTHONY *turns on lamp on his bedside table. Stage lights come up full. Person in downstage corner is a woman in a pink jogging suit, hereafter known as* AUDIENCE.]

NANCY: Shhhh!

ANTHONY: What!?

NANCY: Okay, we're clear. [*She punches button on tape recorder. Music stops. She begins stretching her mouth in various directions, then rattles off some tongue twisters.*] Red leather, yellow leather, red leather, yellow leather, red leath —

ANTHONY: [*Still groggy.*] What are you doing?

NANCY: My lip-loosening exercises.

ANTHONY: Lip —

NANCY: I need to improve my diction …

ANTHONY: Now?

NANCY: … if I want to go national.

ANTHONY: National what?

NANCY: Only syndicated, not network. But the Viacom guy is supposed to come to the show on Thursday, then take a meeting with me.

ANTHONY: What show?

NANCY: Go back to sleep, Tony.

ANTHONY: Who's that woman in the corner?

NANCY: That's the audience.

AUDIENCE: Hi, Nancy! I love you!

NANCY: [*Cooing.*] I love you, too. [*She strikes pose again, for a second.*]

ANTHONY: Audience for what?

NANCY: [*Through her smile.*] My talk show.

ANTHONY: What?

NANCY: "*Nancy After Dark*".

ANTHONY: You ... pfffft ... you don't have a talk show.

NANCY: [*With patronizing patience.*] Practically everybody has a talk show nowadays.

ANTHONY: That's true.

NANCY: There are five in the neighborhood already.

ANTHONY: Five?

NANCY: Marianna's show got axed last week.

ANTHONY: This has got to be a dream ...

NANCY: [*Sharply.*] Yes, it's a dream, go back to sleep.

ANTHONY: Maybe ...

NANCY: We're coming out of commercial soon, so you'll either have to be quiet or pull the covers over your head and *pretend* you're sleeping. You're good at that, aren't you?

AUDIENCE: Go, Nancy!

ANTHONY: How can I sleep with all this talking, and with that woman watching and with the lights on?

NANCY: Look, this is our twenty-third show in the new time slot, and it's the very first time you woke up, so you tell me.

[*Pause.*]

ANTHONY: I don't believe you.

AUDIENCE: [*Calling.*] Hey, Nancy, is that your husband Tony?

ANTHONY: How does she know my name?

NANCY: I talk about you all the time. It's part of my appeal, sort of a Mary Matalin crossed with Erma Bombeck.

ANTHONY: So where's the camera?

NANCY: It's hidden.

ANTHONY: Yeah, right.

NANCY: [*Gesturing.*] In the right eye of ... that red-headed girl ... in the sad eyes painting

ANTHONY: No ... no, it's not. Why am I arguing with you?

NANCY: Alright, it's not. Go back to sleep, Tony.

ANTHONY: Did you ... [*Getting a sudden idea.*] Is this supposed to spice up our sex life?

NANCY: No, but if you have an idea for a show, you can call and leave a message at 1-800-GO-NANCY.

ANTHONY: Alright, alright.

[*He turns off his light, and lays back down.*]

NANCY: [*Strikes a pose. To* AUDIENCE.] We're back ... [AUDIENCE *applauds.*] ... talking about infidelity.

ANTHONY: [*Opening his eyes.*] Infidelity?

NANCY: That's Tony, my husband. [*With an artificial laugh.*] Ha, ha, go back to sleep, honey.

AUDIENCE: [*Calling.*] Go Nancy, Go Nancy ...

NANCY: Our first guest is no stranger to infidelity. Meet Libby.

[AUDIENCE *applauds.* LIBBY *enters, carrying a folding chair, which she opens near* NANCY.]

NANCY: [*Warmly.*] Welcome to my world.

LIBBY: Thank you, Nancy.

[LIBBY *sits.* ANTHONY, *eyes closed, sits up suddenly, "looks" around, then lays back down.*]

NANCY: [*Mouths, to* LIBBY.] That's Tony.

LIBBY: I know.

NANCY: [*Gentle voice.*] So. Tell us what happened.

LIBBY: 'Kay. He was my boss ... [*She sniffs.*] ... At the plant ... [*She sniffs.*]

NANCY: He was your boss at the plant, uh-huh ...

LIBBY: And he'd say nice stuff about my hair and my clothes.

NANCY: That's how it started?

LIBBY: That ... [*Eager to fall in with* NANCY's *scenario.*] ... Yeah! Yeah, that's how it started, Nancy. That's how it started.

NANCY: [*Taking her hand.*] Go on, please.

LIBBY: And one thing led to another.

NANCY: [*Suddenly sassy.*] No, no, girlfriend.

LIBBY: What?

NANCY: I don't think so.

AUDIENCE: Go Nancy, Go Nancy!

LIBBY: Did I do something wrong?

NANCY: [*Warm again.*] We're trying to feel your pain, so be specific.

LIBBY: I'll try.

NANCY: I know you will.

LIBBY: Well ... he went from complimenting my clothes and my hair to complimenting my body.

NANCY: [*Pretending not to understand.*] Your body?

LIBBY: Yes.

NANCY: Well what did he say?

LIBBY: He said ... [*She sniffs.*] ... "Nice rack." Nancy, which part is the rack?

NANCY: And what else?

LIBBY: I don't think I can say the rest of it on television.

NANCY: [*Low.*] We're cable, Libby. That's what cable's for.

LIBBY: [*Quickly.*] Nice jugs, tits, cans, must be a cold day, hey camel toes!

NANCY: So he complimented you and you had sex with him?

LIBBY: Yes. No!

NANCY: No?

LIBBY: That's just how it started. I was trying to explain what he's like.

NANCY: I think we got a pretty good idea of that now, Libby.

LIBBY: The whole picture, I just wanted to give it.

NANCY: You're leaving something out though, aren't you, Libby?

[*Pause.*]

LIBBY: I don't think so.

NANCY: He's married, isn't he?

LIBBY: Yes.

AUDIENCE: Oooooooohh ...

LIBBY: But it wasn't like that.

AUDIENCE: Go Nancy, Go Nancy!

NANCY: Well what was it like? Help us understand.

LIBBY: I didn't know he was married.

NANCY: He never told you ...?

LIBBY: He didn't wear a ring.

NANCY: That's true.

LIBBY: What?

NANCY: We're coming up to a break, so cut to the chase.

LIBBY: He blackmailed me.

NANCY: Really? Wow! How?

LIBBY: He said he'd fire me if I didn't ... submit to him.

NANCY: [Sassy.] Give it up.

LIBBY: What?

NANCY: He wanted you to give it up.

LIBBY: Ye ... Yeah, he wanted me ... He made me give it up, Nancy!

NANCY: Audience, would you like to meet this guy?

AUDIENCE: [Calling.] Yeeesss!

NANCY: Well we will, right after this break.

[NANCY *strikes a pose and holds it for several seconds.* AUDIENCE *applauds wildly.* LIBBY *looks around nervously.*]

NANCY: Okay we're clear.

LIBBY: Nancy, I just want to say thank you —

NANCY: I'm sorry I'm not allowed to talk to you during the break it takes the spontaneity out of the interview.

[LIBBY *nods.*]

NANCY: If you promise to be quick, I'll let you run to the bathroom and get a drink of water.

LIBBY: Uh ... okay. Water's nice.

NANCY: Let me just ... [*She calls towards the bathroom.*] Doctor Bledsoe!

DR. BLEDSOE: [*From offstage, muffled.*] Yes!?

NANCY: She always does this.

DR. BLEDSOE: [*Off.*] I heard that!

LIBBY: I don't really —

DR. BLEDSOE: [*Off.*] No, you can get some water! I'm just putting in my contacts!

LIBBY: It's okay, really.

NANCY: [*Warmly.*] Go-oo!

[LIBBY *exits quickly, taking this as an order.*]

NANCY: [*Quietly.*] What a to-do to die today at a minute or two to two. A thing distinctly hard to say but harder still to do. For —

[AUDIENCE *suddenly rushes up to her with pad and pen.*]

AUDIENCE: Nancy, could I have your autograph?

NANCY: For they'll beat a tattoo — of course ... [*She strikes a pose.*] ... at twenty to two ...

[NANCY *takes pad and pen.* LIBBY *reenters.*]

LIBBY: Okay, I'm ready.

NANCY: Shhh! [*As she signs pad.*] With a ra-ta-ta-ta-ta-ta-ta-ta-tatoo. Sit down, Libby. And the dragon will come when she hears the drum.

DR. BLEDSOE: [*Off.*] What!?

NANCY: Not you! [*She hands pad back to* AUDIENCE. *Under her breath.*] Another dragon.

AUDIENCE: Ooooooh! You're bad, Nancy!

NANCY: I know.

AUDIENCE: I love you, Nancy.

NANCY: [*Striking a pose.*] I love you, too. Now go back to your seat.

[AUDIENCE *returns to seat.*]

NANCY: Sit down, Libby –

[LIBBY *sits.*]

NANCY: Doctor, you're on deck!!

DR. BLEDSOE: [*Off.*] Roger that, Nan!

NANCY: Okay, we're back in five ... [*She strikes a pose.*] ... four ... three ... [*She mouths "two, one."*] ... We're back!

[AUDIENCE *applauds.*]

NANCY: Thank you ... with Libby. Libby has spent some time with our resident therapist and now feels ready to confront the *married* boss that she had an affair with. Isn't that right, Libby?

LIBBY: Yes, Nancy.

NANCY: Audience, are you ready to meet him?

AUDIENCE: Yeeeeess!!

NANCY: Well, I've got a surprise for everybody! [*She hits* ANTHONY.] Wake up!

[ANTHONY *bolts up in bed.* LIBBY *gasps.*]

ANTHONY: What!? [*His eyes are barely open.*]

LIBBY: [*A sad wail.*] Tony ...

NANCY: So now you recognize him?

ANTHONY: [*He turns on bedside lamp. Lights come up full.*] Elizabeth?

LIBBY: [*To* NANCY.] I didn't really look at him before.

ANTHONY: What are you doing here?

LIBBY: [*To* NANCY.] I was talking to you.

NANCY: Thank you.

AUDIENCE: [*Swinging her arm in the air, in the "Arsenio" whoop.*] Whoo whoo whoo whoo whoo whoo ...

NANCY: [*To* AUDIENCE, *instantly plaintive.*] Yes, it's true. Tony is the one. Tony is the adulterer. I am sharing my pain.

AUDIENCE: I love you, Nancy.

NANCY: You're such a comfort.

ANTHONY: How could you do this?

NANCY: It's sweeps week.

ANTHONY: What!?

NANCY: We need to get high ratings.

ANTHONY: How could you do this *to me?*

NANCY: [*Boldly.*] I'm doing it to me, too. My life is an open book. [*To* AUDIENCE.] My life is an open book.

[*Pause.*]

ANTHONY: Maybe you're right.

NANCY: Confession is good for the soul.

ANTHONY: Maybe it's time to get it out in the open.

NANCY: Air our dirty laundry.

LIBBY: Get ... get it off our chests.

NANCY: You look like you did that already, Libby.

AUDIENCE: Go Nancy, Go Nancy.

NANCY: [*Seriously.*] So, Libby, let's first get straight, Tony calls you ... Elizabeth?

LIBBY: It's my professional name.

NANCY: For the plant ... ?

LIBBY: Uh-huh.

NANCY: I thought it was your slut name.

ANTHONY: Nancy!

NANCY: I'm sorry. I don't know what's happening to me. My talk show host self is warring with my talk show guest self, and I feel very volatile ... [*Turning to* AUDIENCE.] ... and you're seeing it live on tape.

AUDIENCE: I love you, Nancy.

DR. BLEDSOE: [*Off.*] Keep going, Nancy! You're finally getting down to the dirty black roots of the problem!

NANCY: [*Brightly.*] And speaking of black roots ...

DR. BLEDSOE: [*Off.*] I heard that!

NANCY: Ah! Our resident therapist, Doctor Allegra Shayne-Bledsoe, who we'll be hearing from ... [*Louder.*] ... in our next segment. But first, Libby, is there anything you'd like to say to Tony?

LIBBY: Yes.

NANCY: Go ahead.

LIBBY: Why did you lie? I feel so guilty, dirty, cheap ...

NANCY: We can all understand that.

LIBBY: Why? [*She sniffs.*] Why?

NANCY: Tony ... why?

ANTHONY: [*As if it's an amazing phenomenon.*] I don't know ... we were drawn together ...

NANCY: It just happened.

ANTHONY: [Amazing, isn't it?] It just happened.

LIBBY: But why? Not how, Tony? Why?

NANCY: Good question, Libby. And we'll answer it right after this break.

[NANCY *strikes a pose, holding it for five seconds.* LIBBY *stares at the floor.* ANTHONY *considers his options.*] We're clear. [*Calling offstage.*] Doctor, get ready!

DR. BLEDSOE: [*Off.*] I have counted the tiles on your shower wall four times! Just introduce me, and don't forget my hyphen.

NANCY: Thirty seconds! [*Fast, to herself.*] If this doctor doctors that doctor —

ANTHONY: Honey —

NANCY: [*Louder.*] Does the doctor doctor the doctor ...

LIBBY: It's no use.

NANCY: The way the doctor he is doctoring doctors doctors ...

LIBBY: She won't let us talk to her during the break.

ANTHONY: Why not?

NANCY: [*Louder.*] Or does the doctor doctor the doctor QUIET! [*She strikes a pose.*] We're back in five, four, three ... [*She mouths "Two, one."*] ... We're back.

[AUDIENCE *applauds.*]

I couldn't get Libby and Tony to talk during the break, but maybe our resident therapist can help. Please welcome Doctor Allegra Shayne-Bledsoe.

[AUDIENCE *applauds.* DR. BLEDSOE *enters, carrying a cushioned chair, which she places next to* TONY. *She stands up straight and takes in the aura of the room.*]

NANCY: Welcome to my world.

DR. BLEDSOE: Thank you, Nancy. I'm feeling a lot of tension in this room.

NANCY: Anger, yes, I can feel it too.

DR. BLEDSOE: No, I think it's sexual tension, Nancy.

NANCY: Sit down, Doctor.

DR. BLEDSOE: [*She sits and takes* ANTHONY'*s hand.*] Tony ... may I call you Tony?

ANTHONY: Yes.

NANCY: There are a few other things I'd like to call you.

AUDIENCE: Go Nancy, G —

DR. BLEDSOE: [*Sharply.*] Please, I'm trying to work here!! [*Kittenishly, to* ANTHONY.] Tony, what do you want?

ANTHONY: A good night's sleep?

DR. BLEDSOE: [*Still kittenish.*] Humor is a very common defense mechanism.

ANTHONY: [*Responding in a similarly sexual way.*] All right. I'd like to put this behind me ...

DR. BLEDSOE: Uh-huh ...

ANTHONY: And get on with my life.

DR. BLEDSOE: [*Squeezing his hand.*] Good work, Tony. That's a very healthy need.

ANTHONY: Thank you.

DR. BLEDSOE: But I think that's up to Libby and Nancy. Gals, what do you think?

AUDIENCE: Throw the bum out!

DR. BLEDSOE: [*Standing.*] HEY!! DO YOU WANNA TRADE PLACES WITH ME?!?! WHAT MEDICAL SCHOOL DID YOU GO TO?!!!!

ANTHONY: Dr. Bledsoe, you're hurting my arm.

DR. BLEDSOE: Just like you hurt Libby and Nancy? [*She lets go of* ANTHONY'*s hand, sits on bed, then crawls across the foot of the bed to* LIBBY.] Libby?

LIBBY: Yes, Doctor?

DR. BLEDSOE: [*Taking* LIBBY'*s hand.*] Do you think you can put this behind you?

LIBBY: I guess so.

DR. BLEDSOE: Good for you.

LIBBY: But what about our baby?

AUDIENCE: Oooooooo!!

LIBBY: [*Crying.*] What about little Toni?

AUDIENCE: Whoop! There it is ... Whoop! There it is ... Wh—

DR. BLEDSOE: [*To* AUDIENCE.] DON'T MAKE ME COME OUT THERE!!! [*To* LIBBY.] You and Tony have a son?

LIBBY: A daughter; Toni with an "i" ya know?

DR. BLEDSOE: How sweet.

LIBBY: She needs her daddy. Tony hasn't seen her in four months, and he hasn't sent us any money in almost a year.

DR. BLEDSOE: How old is little Toni with an "i"?

LIBBY: She'll be two in October.

DR. BLEDSOE: A Libra, I'll bet.

LIBBY: With Sagittarius rising.

[DR. BLEDSOE *releases* LIBBY's *hand and crawls up the bed, squeezing in between* NANCY *and* ANTHONY. *She takes* NANCY's *hand.*]

DR. BLEDSOE: So Nancy ... what are you feeling now?

NANCY: [*To* DR. BLEDSOE.] I'm not sure.
[*To* LIBBY.] Haven't you ever heard of adoption?
[*To* DR. BLEDSOE.] I don't think I'm in touch with my feelings.
[*To* LIBBY.] Haven't you ever heard of birth control?
[*To* DR. BLEDSOE.] No wait ... something's coming.
[*To* LIBBY.] Haven't you ever heard of self-control?
[*To* DR. BLEDSOE.] I feel bad ... angry ... powerless ...

DR. BLEDSOE: That's a start.

NANCY: Hungry ...

DR. BLEDSOE: And what do you want to do?

NANCY: I'd like to kill her ... [This is a guilty pleasure.] ... I think.

DR. BLEDSOE: Uh-huh.

NANCY: Is that wrong?

DR. BLEDSOE: Feelings are not right or wrong. They just are.

NANCY: Well, I do. I feel like killing her ... Doctor?

DR. BLEDSOE: It's extreme.

NANCY: Audience, you say what?

AUDIENCE: Nancy, I think you should kill him, Nancy! He's the one who betrayed you, Nancy.

DR. BLEDSOE: [*To* AUDIENCE.] HOW MANY STATES ARE YOU LICENSED IN?!

NANCY: I don't know ...

AUDIENCE: He's the one you should kill, Nancy!

NANCY: Men stray ... And I think Tony and I have a chance to heal our wounds. Don't you, Tony?

ANTHONY: Absolutely.

DR. BLEDSOE: [*Taking* ANTHONY'*s hand.*] Good.

NANCY: So thank you audience for your feedback, but I'm going to be sticking with Tony, and focussing my revenge on Libby.

DR. BLEDSOE: Good work, Nancy. In the words of Stephen Sondheim, the choice may have been mistaken, but the choosing was not.

NANCY: And unfortunately we're out of time.

DR. BLEDSOE: Awwww.

NANCY: So I guess we'll all have to wait until tomorrow to find out what that revenge is.

DR. BLEDSOE: Well, it is sweeps week.

NANCY: Libby, can you come back tomorrow?

LIBBY: Yeah, I guess so.

AUDIENCE: Wait, this isn't fair! You said you weren't like the others! You said you wouldn't tease us!

NANCY: I won't. I'll do it tomorrow. I promise. Come back tomorrow.

AUDIENCE: I can't come back tomorrow. I'm a guest on "*Desiree 'Til Dawn*" down the street. My husband is a cross-dressing priest.

NANCY: I covered that topic four months ago.

AUDIENCE: The topic of the show is summer fashions. I don't love you anymore, Nancy.

NANCY: All right, all right. Let's compromise.

DR. BLEDSOE: Good choice.

[NANCY *opens drawer of night table, pulls out black glove and puts it on quickly.*]

NANCY: A perfect fit!

AUDIENCE: Go, Nancy.

[NANCY *pulls knife from drawer and stabs* LIBBY *in shoulder.* LIBBY *screams.*]

NANCY: I never could deny my fans anything.

[ANTHONY *jumps out of bed and rushes to help* LIBBY, *who screams again.*]

AUDIENCE: I love you, Nancy.

NANCY: [*To* LIBBY.] Stop being such a baby it's just a flesh wound. [*To* AUDIENCE.] Thanks for coming into my world. I hope you'll visit "*Nancy After Dark*" tomorrow. Sleep tight.

[NANCY *strikes a pose and pushes button on tape recorder. Innocuous music fills stage.* AUDIENCE *applauds and* DR. BLEDSOE *waves and* ANTHONY *helps* LIBBY *offstage as* ...]

Lights Fade.

END OF PLAY

Billy Goda

NO CRIME

Billy Goda

Billy Goda graduated with an MFA in playwrighting from Columbia University in the spring of 1991. Since that time, he has written numerous plays and screenplays while living in the New York community. In 1996, Billy was awarded a Writer's Grant from a private foundation, and in 1999 this grant was renewed as a result of his full length play, *Black Letter Law*, which was inspired by *No Crime*. Billy has received other grants and has had a number of productions in New York City. His most recent work to be seen on the stage, *Nailed Down*, was produced by the "Word of Mouth Theatre Company" of which he is a founding member. Billy's screenplay, *The Cretan Bull*, recently won first prize, out of over eight hundred scripts, in the "New Century Writer Awards" contest.

CHARACTERS:
Cal Roberts, a good looking thirty-year old man.
Jim Abner, a big, egotistical fifty-year old man.

[CAL *is in* JIM ABNER's *office. It is a large office with a great deal of room, light, and a nice view.* JIM *has his cowboy boots up on his desk.*]

JIM: A time comes in a man's life when fifteen minutes can change his future, change his life; these could be your fifteen minutes, Cal.

[*Pause as* JIM *takes a tin of Skoal chewing tobacco out of his desk, packs it down, and takes a dip. He will spit throughout the scene.*]

You're one of three finalists for this position. Now it all depends upon your interview. Whichever one of you has the best interview, that's the one I'll hire. [JIM *spits.*] Nasty habit. I've already met with the other two, so it's up to you now, Cal. It's up to you. [JIM *spits.*] What do you have to say about that?

CAL: I look forward to the challenge ...

JIM: Yeah, yeah, yeah, one of the others said that also. Every time we interview I get that answer: "looking forward to something." You must get it out of a book. Were you reading one of those "what to say in an interview" books?

CAL: I wasn't ...

JIM: I hope not. We need original thinking here. This law firm's been around for fifty-two years, and we've become so damn successful by original thinking; not by memorizing some damn answers in a how to be interviewed book. Are you aware of the success this firm has accomplished?

CAL: I am very aware of that ...

JIM: We've been involved in some of the most important criminal cases in this country, and you know what nearly every one of them have in common? [*Pause.*] I'm asking what do these cases have in common? You said you know about our firm ...

CAL: That you've improved the situation of the defendant. You've either plea bargained for a much lesser charge or you've had your client acquitted.

JIM: That's good, very good. Dave told you to say that, didn't he? [*Laughing.*] That s.o.b.'s ruining all my fun. That question usually scares the pants off the applicant ...

CAL: However, in 1988, the state versus Max Mainer, he received a life sentence. In 1994, Tony Giovano received three consecutive life sentences for multiple murders, and I wonder if you shouldn't have gone with the insanity plea ...

JIM: All right, Cal, you've done your homework; I don't need a history lesson. [*Pause.*] There is only one thing that matters when a client walks through that door. Do you know what that is?

CAL: That he can pay the bill for our legal services.

JIM: [*Laughing.*] Well, yes that too. Make that two things that matter. If he can pay our bill and if there is at least a slight chance of our improving his situation. If there is not that possibility we will reject the case no matter how much money they offer. If you lose cases you lose your reputation. We do not take kindly to losing cases here.

CAL: I understand.

JIM: When we went down with the Giovano fiasco, two very prestigious clients walked out the door with his guilty verdict. [JIM *spits*.] How is Dave?

CAL: He's fine.

JIM: Dave speaks very highly of you.

CAL: Thank you.

JIM: I said Dave does, not me. I don't know you yet. That's one of the main reasons you're sitting in that chair right now — that crazy bastard's a very good friend of mine. At Harvard Law, he saved my butt more than once forcing me to study something other than women and beer. I never understood why he decided to become a professor, without a doubt he could have been one of the top litigates in the country. We could have been partners. [*Pause.*] I have numerous applications with excellent resumes, but you have an ace in your pocket by the name of Dave Horowitz. That recommendation gives you the rail position. What do you have to say about that?

CAL: I think Dave's an excellent judge of character.

JIM: [*Laughing.*] I'm sure you do. He says you'll do whatever it takes to improve your situation — that's the feeling he gets from you. That's an important feeling, very important. What did Dave teach you, Cal? You better not give me a course title.

CAL: How to shoot a gun. How to aim and hit a target.

JIM: Well that's good, but I'm not interviewing you for our rifle team.

CAL: Everyone has a price, that becomes, that is, a weakness, and it's up to me, as a lawyer, as a thinking man, to find out what that is, and then, if need be, to use it. Ready, aim, fire, so to speak.

[*Long pause.*]

[JIM *spits.*]

JIM: A client walks into your office, sits down in your leather arm chair, Cal, lights a cigar, and then tells you the truth of his case, let's say he cracked some lady on the head with a baseball bat splattering her brains all over the sidewalk ... [JIM *spits.*] ... and he played Mickey Mantle on her head because he was ordered to by his, let's call it a supervisor, and he did not question his supervisor's authority. What would you do? How would you feel, Cal? This client has confessed his guilt to you. He has confessed to this horrible, this heinous crime of an innocent lady's head being smashed open. What would you do in defending a client that was guilty, and your only hope of winning the case was by twisting the truth?

[*Long pause.*]

CAL: I cannot accurately answer that question.

JIM: Why not?

CAL: He is my client?

JIM: That's what I said ...

CAL: He has already agreed to use our firm as his representation?

JIM: Correct ...

CAL: He is not guilty.

JIM: Cal, he has confessed to you ...

CAL: He is innocent ...

JIM: He has told you about the murder ...

CAL: He did not commit ...

JIM: He bashed a lady's head in with a bat! Splattering her blood ...

CAL: Blood on the sidewalk from someone else's bat ...

JIM: Are you stupid, son?! What is wrong with you? I have told you, he has told you ...

CAL: You say that my client is guilty, well I say that is impossible, Jim. It is impossible to say he is guilty. He is innocent until someone from the DA's office can persuade a jury of twelve to say he is not innocent. He is innocent until a verdict of guilty is returned. This is why I can not accurately answer your question; this is why your question becomes irrelevant. If he is my client then he is innocent, and it was someone else's bat. Who are the witnesses, Jim? Do you have eyewitnesses? Did he confess to the police? I don't think he confessed or he wouldn't be in my office. Only if he confessed to the police would I start with the idea of his guilt as a possibility. A possibility that I would evaluate and attempt to repudiate. Has our hypothetical client confessed to the police?

JIM: We'll say he has not.

CAL: Then he is not guilty. Then the only thing which can be proved is that some lady's head has been struck with a blunt object causing her death. What other evidence exists, Jim? Is there any other evidence?

[JIM *spits*.]

JIM: Your conscience.

CAL: My conscience is not on trial.

[*Pause.*]

JIM: Would you like a dip of tobacco? Green, Skoal, longcut. Dave's the idiot that started me dipping; he thinks he's a Jewish cowboy from New York. I always chew tobacco when I think — that's as long as no women are around.

CAL: Yes, thank you.

[JIM *passes the tin to* CAL. CAL *packs it down and places a dip in his mouth.*]

JIM: I spit in this bronze cup. It was a present from my daughter. See that: "World's Greatest Dad."

CAL: That's a nice spit cup, sir.

JIM: I never hired a lawyer that dips tobacco.

CAL: It helps me think.

JIM: So your hypothetical client is not guilty?

CAL: No, he isn't.

JIM: I like that answer. I like the logic. The logic of truth not existing until it's been proven again.

CAL: And it can be a very difficult thing to prove.

[*Pause.*]

[JIM *spits and then gives* CAL *an empty cup to spit in.*]

JIM: My instincts seem to be the same as Dave's, and I go with my instincts, Cal. I'm betting you'll be a fine addition to this team.

CAL: Thank you. I'll do my best …

JIM: Is that another answer out of that damn book?

CAL: No, it's not.

JIM: When you start at this firm, you start on probation, so I can see if you have what it takes to succeed.

CAL: That's fine.

JIM: You'll do some leg work for me, gathering some background information. Let's see what questions you come up with, what possibilities you create. [JIM *spits.*] I ask everyone if they'd like a dip of tobacco. No one ever says yes. Most people think it's disgusting.

CAL: Maybe that's why we like it.

JIM: Yes, yes, maybe that is why. I want you to meet someone, Cal. [JIM *buzzes the secretary.*] Send him in.

[*A man enters the office.*]

Cal, this will be your first client. His name is John Stutts. He bashed an elderly lady's head in with a baseball bat.

[*Lights down.*]

END SCENE

Arlene Hutton

I DREAM BEFORE I TAKE THE STAND

For every woman who has ever walked in a park...

Arlene Hutton

Arlene Hutton is a member of New Dramatists, Circle East (formerly Circle Rep Lab) and the Dramatists' Guild. She is resident playwright for The Journey Company, who has produced her work at festivals in the United States and abroad. She is the recipient of a Cameron Mackintosh Foundation grant and the John Lippman Award.

Hutton is the author of *Last Train to Nibroc*, which was a finalist for the Francesca Primus Prize. It was co-produced by The Journey Company/78th Street Theatre Lab at the Assembly Room for the Edinburgh Festival Fringe and Piccolo Spoleto, and moved off-Broadway to the Douglas Fairbanks Theatre, receiving a Drama League nomination for Best Play. Published by Dramatists Play Service, *Last Train to Nibroc* was selected for *Women Playwrights: Best Plays 1999*, and is having a prolific life in regional theatres.

Pushing Buttons was an Actor's Theatre of Louisville 2000 Heineman Award finalist, and two of Hutton's short plays have been Samuel French Short Play Festival winners. *I Dream Before I Take the Stand*, workshopped at Alice's Fourth Floor, was presented by The Journey Company at the Edinburgh Festival Fringe, directed by Judith Royer and featuring Robert Kilbridge and Beth Lincks, who also recorded a special radio version for Stage Shadows, taped live at the Museum of Television and Radio. Hutton's one-acts plays have been presented at university and regional theatres across the country and have been translated into several languages. New York credits include HERE, Circle-in-the-Square Downtown, Neighborhood Playhouse and the West Bank.

Arlene Hutton serves on the Board of Directors of New Dramatists.

CHARACTERS:
She: a petite woman.
He: a man, probably a lawyer.

Casting Note: *The man is age 25-50, the woman 20-50, both of any race. The woman should be petite in height or very slim if taller, but the specific hair color lines may be changed with the author's permission.*

SET: *A chair.*

TIME: *Right now.*

Lights up on a petite woman sitting in a chair. It is possible that the lights begin the play full and soft, narrowing very slowly throughout, so that by the end of the play only a narrow spot is focused on the woman, like an interrogation room. The man, a lawyer, walks around her throughout, at first in the full circle or light, later appearing in and out of the focused light. Perhaps by the end of the play, the light has narrowed on the woman, and the man is barely seen. There are many ways to present this play, but the pauses are a part of the dialogue.

SHE: I was walking through the park.

HE: Why were you in the park?

SHE: I was on my way to work.

HE: Do you have to walk through the park to get to work?

SHE: No.

HE: Do you always walk through the park to work?

SHE: No.

HE: Why did you walk through the park that day?

SHE: It was a beautiful day. I like to walk to work through the park when the weather's good.

[*Pause.*]

HE: Were you in a hurry?

SHE: I was on my way to work.

HE: Were you late?

SHE: No, I would have been on time.

HE: Were you strolling or walking fast?

SHE: I always walk fairly quickly.

HE: Why? The park is not safe?

SHE: I guess not.

HE: Yet you walk through it to get to work.

SHE: There are lots of people around.

HE: But you walk quickly through the park.

SHE: Yes.

[*Pause.*]

HE: How do you walk?

SHE: Which way?

HE: Do you swing your arms?

SHE: I don't know.

HE: Were you carrying anything?

SHE: Just my purse.

HE: So your arms were free to swing along as you walked.

SHE: Maybe.

HE: Or maybe you walk with them folded.

SHE: I don't know what you mean.

HE: Perhaps you fold your arms.

[*He demonstrates.*]

SHE: Maybe.

HE: So sometimes you swing your arms and sometimes you fold them.

SHE: I guess.

HE: What else would you do with them?

SHE: I guess you're right.

[*Pause.*]

HE: So you were walking through the park that day on your way to work.

SHE: Yes. I already said that.

[*Pause.*]

HE: What were you wearing?

SHE: A skirt and a top.

HE: What color was the skirt?

SHE: It was a print.

HE: What color?

SHE: Black and red.

HE: And the top?

SHE: What?

HE: What color was the top?

SHE: Black.

HE: Just black?

SHE: It had a little red flower on it.

HE: The fabric?

SHE: No. A decoration.

HE: Where?

SHE: In the center of the neckline.

HE: A rose.

SHE: I guess. It was tiny.

HE: It was in the fabric?

SHE: No. It was a small ribbon.

HE: Like the little flowers on lingerie.

SHE: Like that.

HE: How sweet. [*A pause.*] Were you wearing jewelry?

SHE: No. Just a watch.

HE: An expensive watch?

SHE: No.

HE: An expensive *looking* watch?

SHE: No. Just a Timex.

HE: So that you could hurry through the park to be at work on time.

SHE: Of course.

HE: No other jewelry?

SHE: No.

HE: Why not?

SHE: I don't wear jewelry in the park.

HE: Why not?

SHE: I don't want to attract attention.

HE: You don't want to get mugged.

SHE: Right.

> [*Pause.*]

HE: Your hair is up today. Were you wearing it that way in the park?

SHE: No. I was wearing it down.

HE: Why?

SHE: It probably wasn't quite dry.

HE: You go out with wet hair? Why?

SHE: In nice weather.

HE: Why?

SHE: It feels good.

HE: And you color your hair.

SHE: Yes.

HE: And why is that?

SHE: I like it.

HE: Why? What is your natural color?

SHE: Like this when I was in college.

HE: But now?

SHE: I don't know.

HE: You don't know what color your hair is?

SHE: It's been a while —

HE: What color do you think it is?

SHE: I imagine it's sort of a dirty blonde with a little gray. [Note: *"dirty blonde" can be "mousy brown," depending on the hair color of the actress. "With a little gray" can be omitted.*]

HE: But you don't really know.

SHE: Not really.

HE: [*Optional pause.*] Do you think you are more attractive with colored hair?

SHE: I don't know.

HE: Then why do you color it?

SHE: I guess so.

HE: What?

SHE: I guess I think I'm —

HE: So you color your hair to be more attractive.

SHE: I guess.

HE: But your fingernails are not painted.

SHE: No.

HE: Do you sometimes paint your fingernails?

SHE: Sometimes I wear nail polish.

HE: Were your fingernails painted that day?

SHE: I think so.

HE: What nail color did you use?

SHE: A pink polish.

HE: Not red.

SHE: No. Just pink.

HE: Why?

SHE: To match my make-up.

HE: You were wearing make-up?

SHE: Yes.

HE: Do you always wear make-up to the park?

SHE: No.

HE: They why were you wearing it that day?

SHE: I was on my way to work.

HE: What sort of make-up were you wearing?

SHE: What brand?

HE: Which items of make-up had you put on? Lipstick?

SHE: Yes.

HE: What color?

SHE: The actual name?

HE: What color would *you* call the lipstick you wore?

SHE: A sort of peach, maybe, with a darker —

HE: You were wearing two colors on your lips?

SHE: Well, yes.

HE: How does one do that?

SHE: It's a lip liner with a brush and then a tube lipstick.

HE: You outline your lips before you put on your lipstick.

SHE: Yes. It's —

HE: You add definition to your lips.

SHE: Sort of.

HE: To emphasize them. You emphasize your lips.

SHE: It's just the way you put on make-up.

[*Possibly a pause.*]

HE: What other make-up were you wearing?

SHE: A little powder.

HE: Why?

SHE: So my nose wouldn't be shiny.

HE: And why would it?

SHE: It was a fairly warm day.

HE: You might have perspired a little.

SHE: Maybe.

HE: And was there color on your cheeks?

SHE: Yes. I use a little blush.

HE: Color on the eyes?

SHE: Eyeliner. Maybe a little eye shadow.

HE: Mascara.

SHE: No.

HE: Are you sure?

SHE: Yes. I don't use mascara.

HE: Why not?

SHE: It bothers my contact lenses.

HE: Were you wearing contact lenses in the park?

SHE: Yes.

HE: You weren't wearing glasses?

SHE: No.

HE: But you are wearing glasses now.

SHE: Sometimes I wear contact lenses.

HE: You were wearing contact lenses in the park.

SHE: I already said that.

HE: Your hair was down and you were wearing make-up and contact lenses.

SHE: I already said that.

HE: Your hair was down and you were wearing make-up and contact lenses.

SHE: Yes.

[*A pause.*]

HE: Were you wearing perfume?

SHE: Cologne.

HE: Do you always wear perfume?

SHE: Cologne. I was wearing cologne.

HE: Do you always wear cologne?

SHE: Usually.

HE: In the park?

SHE: To work.

HE: And it was a warm day.

SHE: Yes. But what does that—

HE: You were walking through the park on your way to work dressed in your skirt and top. Your hair was down and you were wearing make-up and perfume.

SHE: Cologne.

[*A long pause. She has won this round, and he must regroup.*]

HE: You were walking through the park.

SHE: Yes.

HE: You passed a man sitting on a bench.

SHE: [*After a slight pause.*] There were lots of people sitting on benches.

HE: You passed many people.

SHE: Yes.

HE: The park was crowded.

SHE: No.

HE: The park was not empty.

SHE: No. But there were a lot of people.

HE: Did you see anyone you knew?

SHE: No.

HE: No neighbors or friends or familiar faces?

SHE: No.

HE: You walked past the people sitting on benches.

SHE: Yes.

HE: There was a man sitting on a bench by himself.

SHE: I didn't notice he was alone.

HE: He spoke to you.

SHE: Yes.

HE: You spoke to him.

SHE: No.

HE: He spoke to you.

SHE: Yes.

HE: What did he say?

SHE: He just said hello.

HE: And what did you do?

SHE: I nodded to him and kept on walking.

HE: Did you know him?

SHE: No.

HE: Had you ever seen him before?

SHE: No.

HE: He was a stranger.

SHE: Yes.

HE: Yet you nodded at him. Did you smile as you nodded?

SHE: Yes.

HE: Why?

SHE: It was a beautiful day. I was just passing by and he said hello.

HE: Do you always acknowledge comments from strangers on the street?

SHE: Not always.

HE: Then why did you acknowledge this man?

SHE: It was such a nice day. And I don't like to be rude.

HE: So this stranger said hello and you smiled and nodded.

SHE: That's right.

HE: Did you speak to other people sitting on the benches?

SHE: No.

HE: Did you speak to anyone else in the park?

SHE: No.

HE: Why not?

SHE: No one else spoke to me.

HE: But when a strange man said hello you smiled and nodded at him.

SHE: Yes. There were lots of people —

HE: Did you stop to smile and nod?

SHE: What?

HE: Did you stop still in front of the man to smile at him?

SHE: No. I kept walking.

HE: Why didn't you stop?

SHE: I didn't think about it. It was just a casual hello. I just kept walking. It was nothing.

HE: Not really. [*Pause.*] What were you wearing?

SHE: What?

HE: What were you wearing?

SHE: I told you.

HE: You have to answer. What were you wearing?

SHE: A skirt and a top.

HE: To go to work?

SHE: I had a jacket in the office.

HE: What kind of skirt?

SHE: A printed one.

HE: A red and black print.

SHE: Yes.

HE: Was it long or short?

SHE: What?

HE: The skirt. Was it below your knees?

SHE: No.

HE: It came above your knees.

SHE: Yes.

HE: It was tight. It clung to your body?

SHE: No. It was gathered. A full skirt.

HE: So it might have moved when you walked.

SHE: I don't know.

HE: What was the fabric?

SHE: Chiffon.

HE: Chiffon is a sheer fabric.

SHE: It was lined.

HE: What was the lining?

SHE: The lining was chiffon, too.

HE: So you were wearing a see-through mini skirt.

SHE: No.

HE: Describe the blouse.

SHE: What?

HE: You were wearing a top.

SHE: Yes. A T-shirt.

HE: A knit top.

SHE: Yes.

HE: Did it have sleeves?

SHE: No. It was sleeveless.

HE: A tank top. It was tight.

SHE: No.

HE: It fitted closely on your body. What color was it?

SHE: I already told you.

HE: What color was it?

SHE: [*An outburst.*] Black.

HE: With a little red flower. [*Possibly a pause.*] Were you wearing underwear?

SHE: [*Surprised at this question.*] Yes.

HE: Were you wearing a slip?

SHE: No.

HE: Why not?

SHE: It was warm out. And the skirt was lined.

HE: Were you wearing panty hose?

SHE: No.

HE: Your legs were bare.

SHE: Yes.

HE: No socks?

SHE: I told you. I was wearing sandals.

HE: For the office?

SHE: I keep stockings and pumps in my desk.

HE: Along with a jacket.

SHE: Yes.

HE: You walk through the park half naked and cover up for the office.

SHE: [*After a pause.*] It's air-conditioned.

HE: What?

SHE: The office. It's air-conditioned. It gets cold.

HE: But the park was hot.

SHE: Yes.

HE: So you don't wear much clothing. Were your legs shaved?

SHE: Yes.

HE: Why do you shave your legs?

SHE: I just do.

HE: It looks better.

SHE: Yes.

HE: So you weren't wearing pantyhose.

SHE: I already said that.

HE: No stockings at all.

SHE: I was wearing sandals.

HE: Were you wearing a bra?

SHE: What?

HE: Were you wearing a bra?

SHE: Yes.

HE: What size?

SHE: Thirty-four.

HE: Thirty-four what?

SHE: Just thirty-four.

HE: What cup size are you?

SHE: Um, uh, B or C.

HE: You don't know?

SHE: It depends on the bra. What brand.

HE: What was the cup size of the bra you had on that day?

SHE: It didn't have a cup size. It was just a 34.

HE: Why didn't it have a cup size? Don't most bras have a cup size?

SHE: It wasn't sized that way. It didn't have an underwire.

HE: So it was an elastic sort of bra.

SHE: I don't know. Maybe.

[*A slight pause.*]

HE: How tall are you?

SHE: Five foot three.

HE: You are considered a petite woman, then.

SHE: I guess so.

HE: But thirty-four B or C is a fairly large bra size for a small woman.

SHE: It's average.

HE: Not for a petite woman. You wouldn't say your breasts were small.

SHE: My ...

HE: Your breasts. They are not small breasts.

SHE: I don't know.

HE: You don't know you have large breasts?

SHE: They're average.

HE: Do you always wear a bra?

SHE: When?

HE: When you walk through the park, do you always wear a bra?

SHE: Yes.

HE: Why?

SHE: I feel more comfortable.

HE: Because you have large breasts.

SHE: [*No answer.*]

HE: You would not say that you have small breasts.

SHE: No ...

HE: You have a large bust. But you were wearing a tank top.

SHE: It was hot.

HE: You were wearing a tight T-shirt. How wide were the straps on your tank top?

SHE: I don't know.

HE: Wide enough to cover the bra straps?

SHE: Well, yes.

HE: You were carrying a purse.

SHE: Yes.

HE: What kind?

SHE: A small leather one.

HE: You were carrying it in your hand.

SHE: No.

HE: It had a strap.

SHE: Yes.

HE: How were you carrying your purse?

SHE: On my shoulder. The strap was on my shoulder.

HE: Could it cause your tank top strap to shift?

SHE: What?

HE: The strap on your tank top. Could your purse strap have caused it to shift?

SHE: I guess.

HE: Revealing your bra strap.

SHE: Maybe.

HE: So your bra straps could have been showing as you walked through the park.

SHE: I don't know.

[*Pause.*]

HE: What color was your underwear?

SHE: What does it matter?

HE: What color was your underwear?

SHE: [*Overlapping.*] Black.

HE: The bra or the panties?

SHE: Both.

HE: They matched?

SHE: Yes.

HE: Did they have lace?

SHE: Yes.

HE: You were wearing a black lacy bra and panties?

SHE: That's right.

HE: Why not white or beige?

SHE: To match the tank top and skirt.

HE: Why? Did you expect anyone to see your underwear that day?

SHE: What?

HE: [*Doesn't answer.*]

SHE: No.

HE: Did you have a date with a boyfriend later?

SHE: No.

HE: Then why did it have to match?

SHE: What?

HE: The underwear. The bra and panties.

SHE: In case it ... in case the tank strap ...

HE: So you expected the bra strap to be seen.

SHE: Not necessarily.

HE: But you thought it might.

SHE: I didn't really think about it. It's just what I put on that morning.

HE: Black lacy underwear is considered sexy.

SHE: I guess.

HE: It is sexier than white or beige.

SHE: I guess so.

HE: Black is considered a sexy color. So is red.

SHE: I don't know.

HE: Your skirt was black and red. Your top was black with a little red ribbon flower on it. Your bra and panties were black.

SHE: That's right.

HE: So why were you wearing sexy underwear if no one was to see it?

SHE: I just like it.

HE: Why?

SHE: It makes me feel ...

HE: Sexier.

SHE: Prettier.

HE: More sensual.

SHE: More feminine.

HE: You walked through the park wearing sexy underwear and revealing clothes and you smiled and nodded at a man you did not know.

SHE: No.

HE: No?

SHE: Not like that.

HE: You walked through the park.

SHE: Yes.

HE: You were wearing black lacy underwear.

SHE: Yes.

HE: You were wearing a tight tank top and a see-through skirt.

SHE: I ...

HE: You nodded at a strange man.

SHE: Okay.

HE: You smiled at him.

SHE: Okay.

HE: Your bra strap had slipped, and you felt sexy.

SHE: No.

HE: It was a hot day.

SHE: Yes.

HE: Your legs were bare. Your thighs were warm.

SHE: No.

HE: The weather was warm.

SHE: Yes.

HE: You were walking quickly.

SHE: Yes.

HE: You worked up a sweat.

SHE: I don't know.

HE: It is likely you were perspiring.

SHE: I guess.

HE: Your clothes were clinging to you.

SHE: No.

HE: You were moist with sweat and the chiffon lining of your skirt was clinging to your legs as you walked. Your knit top was damp and clung closely to your body.

SHE: That's not right.

HE: It was a hot day. You were walking quickly. You were perspiring.

SHE: [*No answer.*]

HE: Your clothes were warm and sticky. The shape of your body was revealed. Have your breasts been artificially enlarged?

SHE: No.

HE: Or reduced?

SHE: No.

HE: They have not been altered in any way.

SHE: No.

HE: So your breasts are not, shall we say, unnaturally firm.

SHE: I guess not.

HE: And your bra had no underwire.

SHE: We've been through that.

HE: So your breasts had little support.

SHE: I was wearing a bra.

HE: You were walking quickly.

SHE: Yes.

HE: Your breasts were bouncing.

SHE: I don't know.

HE: Your strap might have slipped. Your breasts had no support.

SHE: I was wearing a bra.

HE: You were swinging your arms.

SHE: You said that.

HE: You were either swinging your arms or your arms were folded holding up your breasts.

SHE: I don't know.

HE: Tank tops are low cut.

SHE: It wasn't really —

HE: You folded your arms under your breasts to show your cleavage.

SHE: No.

HE: Might you have folded your arms?

SHE: Not to —

HE: Is it possible you folded your arms?

SHE: Maybe.

HE: Or you were swinging your arms?

SHE: No.

HE: You were walking quickly.

SHE: Yes. To —

HE: Then you were swinging your arms.

SHE: I don't know.

HE: You were swaying your hips.

SHE: No.

HE: You were swinging your arms and your breasts were bouncing.

SHE: No.

HE: Your large breasts were bouncing and your strap was showing.

SHE: No.

HE: If you were walking at a fast pace your breasts would bounce and your hips sway.

SHE: I didn't think about it.

HE: That's right. [*Pause.*] What size panties?

SHE: What?

HE: What size were your panties?

SHE: Medium, I guess.

HE: You don't know?

SHE: I don't remember.

HE: What size panties do you usually buy?

SHE: Medium or small. It depends.

HE: On what?

SHE: On what's on sale, the style, I don't know.

HE: What style?

SHE: I don't know what you mean.

HE: What style were those panties? Bikini panties?

SHE: That's right.

HE: Why?

SHE: Why what?

HE: Why were you wearing bikini panties?

SHE: They matched the bra.

HE: Wouldn't a looser fitting panty be more comfortable?

SHE: Not really.

HE: Bikini panties allow your thighs to touch each other.

SHE: Stop it.

HE: It was a very hot day. You walked quickly through the park wearing sexy clothes with your breasts bouncing and your thighs damp and you smiled and nodded at a stranger.

SHE: That's not it.

HE: You were walking through the park.

SHE: Yes.

HE: It was a hot day.

SHE: Yes.

HE: You smiled at a stranger. And he followed you.

SHE: I didn't know.

HE: What?

SHE: I didn't know that he had followed me.

HE: When did you notice that he followed you?

SHE: When he grabbed me.

HE: Not before?

SHE: He grabbed me from behind. I didn't see him.

HE: You didn't turn when you heard someone behind you?

SHE: There was loud music. I didn't hear anything.

HE: The music was so loud you didn't hear someone behind you?

SHE: There was a machine ...

HE: A lawnmower?

SHE: Louder. An edger. There was loud music and loud noise. I didn't
hear him.

HE: You went into the park.

SHE: To walk to work.

HE: You were wearing suggestive clothing.

SHE: No.

HE: You signaled to a man.

SHE: No.

HE: You enticed him.

SHE: No.

HE: You led him on.

SHE: No.

HE: You acknowledged him.

SHE: [*No answer.*]

HE: You smiled at him.

SHE: Yes.

[*The lights are beginning to dim, leaving an ever-brightening single spot focused in the woman's eyes, like an interrogation room. Perhaps the man fades into the background during the rest of the play. Or maybe not.*]

HE: [*He verbally rapes her.*] You left your glasses off. Your dyed hair was bobbing in the breeze. You had painted nails and wore rouge. Your body was scented. You were wearing a revealing outfit, you were feeling sexy in your dainty black lacy undies and your tight shirt and your sheer skirt, and you were shaking your breasts and rolling your hips at this man.

SHE: [*Quite possibly a scream.*] No!

[*A very long pause.*]

HE: Start at the beginning.

SHE: What?

HE: Start at the beginning.

SHE: I was walking through the park.

HE: And?

SHE: It was a nice day. [*Pause.*] It was a nice day.

[*Blackout.*]

END OF PLAY

Tony Kushner

REVERSE TRANSCRIPTION

SIX PLAYWRIGHTS BURY A SEVENTH

A Ten-Minute Play that's nearly Twenty Minutes Long

Tony Kushner

Tony Kushner's plays include *A Bright Room Called Day*; *The Illusion*, freely adapted from Corneille; *Angels In America, A Gay Fantasia on National Themes, Part One: Millennium Approaches* and *Part Two: Perestroika*; *Reverse Transcription* (a one act); *Slavs!: Thinking About the Longstanding Problems of Virtue and Happiness*, *Hydriotaphia*, *Homebody/Kabul*, and adaptations of Goethe's *Stella*, Brecht's *The Good Person of Setzuan*, and Ansky's *A Dybbuk*. His work has been produced at theatres around the United States, including New York Theatre Workshop, the New York Shakespeare Festival, The Mark Taper Forum, Berkeley Repertory, Steppenwolf Theatre, and Hartford Stage Company; on Broadway at the Walter Kerr Theatre; at the Royal National Theatre in London, The Abbey Theatre in Dublin, The Deutsche Theatre in Berlin, and in over thirty countries around the world. *Angels in America* has been awarded the 1993 Pulitzer Prize for Drama, the 1993 and 1994 Tony Awards for Best Play, the 1993 and 1994 Drama Desk Awards, the 1992 Evening Standard Award, two Olivier Award nominations, the 1993 New York Drama Critics Circle Award, the 1993 Los Angles Drama Critics Circle Award, and the 1994 LAMBDA Literary Award for Drama, among others. Mr. Kushner is the recipient of grants from New York State Council on the Arts and the National Endowment for the Arts, a 1990 Whiting Foundation Writer's Award, and an Arts Award from the American Academy of Arts and Letters, among others. Currently, Mr. Kushner is working on a film about Eugene O'Neill for Scott Rudin and a musical theatre piece entitled *Caroline Or Change*. Mr. Kushner was born in Manhattan and grew up in Lake Charles, Louisiana. He has a B.A. from Columbia University and an M.F.A. in directing from NYU, where he studied with Carl Weber. He lives in Manhattan.

Reverse Transcription premiered at Actors Theatre of Louisville's 1996 Humana Festival.

CAST:

HAUTFLOTE: a playwright in his late thirties. He writes beautiful plays everyone admires; he has a following and little financial success. He was DING's best friend, the executor of his will and his wishes.

ASPERA: a playwright in her early thirties. She writes fierce, splendidly intelligent, challenging plays, frequently with lesbian characters, and cannot get an American theater to produce her for love or money. So she lives in London, where she is acclaimed. She is cool and is beginning to sound British.

BIFF: a playwright in his late thirties. Scruffy, bisexual, one success, several subsequent failures, cannot stay away from political themes though his analysis is not rigorous. He is overdue; he should be home, writing; he should not be here.

HAPPY: a playwright in his late thirties. His early plays were widely admired, then one big success and he's become a Hollywood writer, TV mostly, rich now, a little bored, but very happy. He plans to go back to writing for the theater someday.

OTTOLINE: a playwright in her fifties. African-American, genuinely great, hugely influential experimentalist whom everyone adores but who is now languishing in relative obscurity and neglect, though she continues to write prolifically. She is the best writer of the bunch and the least well remunerated. Hers is a deep bitterness; the surface is immensely gracious. She teaches playwrights and has a zoological fascination, watching them. DING was her protege, sort of. She is an old friend of FLATTY's.

FLATTY: a playwright in his late forties. Colossally rich. An easy target for negativity of all kinds though he is in fact a good writer, hugely prolific, very hard-working and generous to his fellow 'wrights.

DING: A dead playwright wrapped in a winding sheet. A very talented writer, whom everyone admired for wildly different reasons.

The play takes place in Abel's Hill cemetery on Abel's Hill, Martha's Vineyard, in December near midnight. Abel's Hill is a real place, a spectacularly beautiful, mostly nineteenth-century Yankee graveyard; it's way too expensive for any mortal to get a plot in it now. Lillian Hellman and Dashiell Hammett are buried there. So is John Belushi, whose tombstone kept getting stolen by fans till Dan Aykroyd put a gigantic boulder on Belushi's grave, too huge for anyone to lift. From the crest of the hill you can see the ocean.
Everyone has shovels, and several have bottles of various liquors.
The night is beautiful and very cold.
They are writers, so they love words. Their speech is precise, easy, articulate; they are showing off a little. They are at that stage of drunk, right before sloppy, where you are eloquent, impressing yourself. They are making pronouncements, aware of their wit; this mustn't be pinched, crabbed, dour, effortful. They are having fun on this mad adventure; they relish its drama. Underneath is a very deep grief.

They all really loved Ding.

[High atop Abel's Hill, a cemetery on Martha's Vineyard. Just athwart the crest. Tombstones all around. As the voice of the playwright is heard on tape, with an accompanying obbligato of a typewriter's clattering, BIFF, HAPPY, ASPERA, OTTOLINE, *and* FLATTY *gather, facing downhill.* HAUTFLOTE *appears, carrying the body of* DING, *wrapped in a winding sheet.* HAUTFLOTE *places the body before them, then runs off, then returns with six shovels. The other playwrights look about uneasily, and then sit. They have come to bury him illegally. It's nearly midnight.]*

THE VOICE OF THE PLAYWRIGHT: Dramatis Personae: Seven characters, all playwrights. BIFF, scruffy, bisexual, one success, several subsequent failures, cannot stay away from political themes though his analysis is not rigorous. He is overdue; he should be home, writing; he should not be here. HAPPY, his early plays were widely admired, then one big success and he's become a Hollywood writer, TV mostly, rich now, a little bored, but very ... um, well, happy. He plans to go back to writing for the theater someday. APSERA writes fierce, splendidly intelligent, challenging plays, frequently with lesbian characters, and she cannot get an American theater to produce her for love or money. So she lives in London where she is acclaimed. OTTOLINE, African-American, genuinely great, hugely influential experimentalist whom everyone adores but who is now languishing in relative obscurity and neglect, the best writer of the bunch and the least well remunerated. She is an old friend of FLATTY, colossally successful, colossally rich. An easy target for negativity of all kinds though he is in fact a good writer, hugely prolific. HAUTFLOTE, writes experimental plays, has a small loyal following and little financial success; the best friend and executor of the estate of DING, a dead playwright wrapped in a winding sheet, very talented, whom everyone admired for wildly different reasons. Seven characters are too many for a ten-minute play. It'll be twenty minutes long! Fuck it. One of them is dead and the others can all talk fast. The play takes place in Abel's Hill cemetery, a spectacularly beautiful mostly nineteenth-century Yankee graveyard, way too expensive for any mortal to get a plot in it now. On Abel's Hill, Martha's Vineyard, in December near midnight.

[*When the voice is finished*, HAUTFLOTE *goes to a nearby headstone, on the side of which is a light switch. He flicks it on; a full moon appears in the sky.*]

HAUTFLOTE: Ah!

[*The play begins.*]

HAUTFLOTE: Here. We should start digging.

ASPERA: Athwart the crest. Facing the sea. As Ding demanded.

OTTOLINE: Isn't this massively illegal?

FLATTY: Trespass, destruction of private property, destruction of a historical landmark I shouldn't wonder, conveyance of tissue, i.e. poor Ding, in an advanced state of morbidity, on public transportation ...

HAUTFLOTE: He's been *preserved*. He's hazardous to no one's health. He traveled here in a steamer trunk. The porters helped.

BIFF: [*Apostrophizing.*] O please come to me short sweet simple perfect *idea*. A seed, a plot.

HAUTFLOTE: He's under a deadline.

BIFF: I'm doomed.

HAUTFLOTE: Now shoulder your shovels ...

BIFF: There's no dignity, have you noticed? In being *this*. An American playwright. What is that?

OTTOLINE: Well, we drink.

HAPPY: No one really drinks now. None of us, at least not publicly.

FLATTY: I can't remember something.

HAPPY : We're ... [*Looking for the word.*]

FLATTY: A name.

HAPPY: Healthier!

HAUTFLOTE: What name?

FLATTY: The name of the country that makes me despair.

HAPPY: But tonight we are drunk.

BIFF: In honor of Ding.

HAUTFLOTE: What letter does it begin with?

BIFF: Poor Ding.

[*They all look at* DING. *Little pause.*]

ASPERA: "And Poor Ding Who Is Dead."

[*Little pause. They all look at* DING.]

FLATTY: R.

HAUTFLOTE: Rwanda.

FLATTY: *That's* it.

OTTOLINE:. How could you *forget*, Flatty? Rwanda?

FLATTY: I've never had a head for names. Not in the news much anymore, Rwanda.

OTTOLINE: We are afraid to stick the shovel in.

HAUTFLOTE: Yes.

OTTOLINE: Believing it to be a desecration.

HAUTFLOTE: Of this holy earth.

OTTOLINE: Not *holy*: Pure. Authentic.

HAPPY: Yankee.

OTTOLINE: Pilgrim.

HAPPY: Puritan.

OTTOLINE: Forefatherly. Originary.

ASPERA: Oh fuck me, "originary"; John Belushi's buried here!

FLATTY: And he had enough drugs in him when he died to poison all the waters from here to Nantucket.

OTTOLINE: And the people steal his tombstone.

FLATTY: No!

OTTOLINE: Or the hill keeps swallowing it up. It doesn't rest in peace. A pretender, you see.

ASPERA: Lillian Hellman's buried here. She's a playwright.

HAUTFLOTE: Appropriate or no, it's what Ding wanted.

OTTOLINE: And that's another thing. It cost two hundred thirty-seven dollars and fifty cents for a round trip ticket. From New York. This is an *island*. Martha's Vineyard is an *island!* Did Ding *realize* that? One has to *ferry* across. Fucking Ding. Maybe *you all* have money. For ferry passage. I don't have money. I've got no money.

FLATTY: I told you I'd pay for you.

OTTOLINE: Well we all know *you've* got money.

BIFF: O come to me short sweet simple idea!

FLATTY: I want something magical to happen.

BIFF: A plot. The Horseleech hath two daughters. It's a start. And these daughters ... Do ... What?

HAPPY: They cry!

OTTOLINE: Give, give!

BIFF: Brecht in exile circumnavigated the globe. Berlin. Skovsbostrand. Stockholm. Helsinki. Leningrad. Moscow. Vladivostok. Manila. L.A. Quick stop in D.C. to visit the HUAC. New York. Paris. Zurich. Salzburg. Prague. Berlin. An American playwright, what is that? Never in exile, always in extremis. The list of cities: AIDS, loss, fear of infection, unsafe sex he says gazing upon the corpse of a fallen comrade, I fuck men and women. I dream my favorite actor has been shot by the police, I dream I shoot Jesse Helms in the head and it doesn't kill him ...

FLATTY: Eeewww, *politics.*

BIFF: I dream we are intervening in Bosnia merely to give Germany hegemony over Eastern Europe. Why, I dream myself in my dream asking myself, do you dream that? You do not dream a play, you *write* a play. And this play is due, and there's [*Pointing to* DING'*s corpse.*] the deadline. I write in my notebook that I am glad we are sending troops to former Yugoslavia but I [*He makes the "in quotes" gesture with his fingers.*] "inadvertently" spell troops "T-R-O-U-P-E-S" as in troupes as in theatrical troupes, traveling players, we are sending *troupes* to former Yugoslavia.

HAUTFLOTE: I don't think we can avoid it any longer. The digging.

FLATTY: I imagine it's worth serious jail time for us all.

HAPPY: Incarcerated playwrights. Now *that* has dignity. Until it's learned what for.

BIFF: I repulse myself, I am not of this earth; if I were more serious I would be an essayist if I were more observant a novelist more articulate more intelligent a poet more ... succinct more *ballsy* a screenwriter and then I could buy an apartment.

HAUTFLOTE: Fuck the public. It's all Ding asked for. He never got his own, alive.

ASPERA: Poor poor Ding.

HAUTFLOTE: He grew obsessed with this cemetery, in his final months. We visited it years ago. On a day trip, we could never afford … to *stay* here. Or anywhere. Or anything. Health insurance. "Bury me on Abel's Hill." His final words. I think he thought this place would give him a retroactive pedigree.

OTTOLINE: That's it, *pedigree*, not *holiness*. Blood, genes. Of which we playwrights are envious. We're mutts. Amphibians.

ASPERA: Not of the land not of the sea. Not of the page nor of the moment.

HAPPY: Perdurable page. Fleeting moment.

FLATTY: Something magical should happen now.

HAUTFLOTE: Ding wanted to belong. Or rather, he never wanted not to. Or rather he never didn't want to, he *wanted* to not want to, but did. In his final months he grew finical.

ASPERA: When I saw him he wasn't finical, he was horrible. He looked horrible and he screamed at everyone all day and all night and there was no way he could get warm, ever. It was quite a change. I hadn't seen him in months, I was visiting from London, WHERE I LIVE, *IN EXILE*, PRODUCED, APPLAUDED, *LAUDED* EVEN and NO ONE IN AMERICA WILL **TOUCH** MY WORK, but anyway he was somehow very very angry but not bitter. One felt envied, but not blamed. At Ding's deathbed.

HAUTFLOTE: Ding Bat. Der Dingle. Ding-an-Sich.

HAPPY: I remember being impressed when I learned that the HIV virus, which has robbed us of our Ding, reads and writes its genetic alphabets backwards, RNA transcribing DNA transcribing RNA, hence *retro*virus, reverse transcription. I'm not gay but I am a Jew and so of course I, too, "read backwards, write backwards"; I think of Hebrew.

FLATTY: You're not gay?

HAPPY: No.

FLATTY: You're *not?*

HAPPY: No.

FLATTY: Everyone thinks you are. Everyone wants to sleep with you. Everyone. *Everyone.*

Oops.

You were saying?

HAPPY: I was saying that in my grief I thought ... Well here I attempt a metaphor doomed to fail ... I mean here we are, playwrights in a graveyard, here to dig, right? So, digging, I think: HIV, reverse transcribing, dust to dust, writing backwards, Hebrew and the Great and Terrible magic of that backwards alphabet, which runs against the grain, counter to the current of European tradition, heritage, thought: a language of fiery, consuming revelation, of refusal, the proper way, so I was taught, to address oneself to God ... [*He puts his hands on* DING'*s body.*] Perhaps, maybe, this backwards-writing viral nightmare is keeping some secret, subterraneanly affianced to a principle of ... Reversals: good reversals and also very bad, where good meets bad, perhaps, the place of mystery where back meets forth, where our sorrow's not the point, where the forward flow of life brutally throws itself into reverse, to reveal ... [*He lies alongside the body, curls up to it, head on* DING'*s shoulder, listening.*] What? Hebrew always looked to me like zipper teeth unzipped. What awesome thing is it we're zipping open? To what do we return when we write in reverse? What's relinquished, what's released?

What does it sound like I'm doing here?

ASPERA: It sounds like you're equating Hebrew and AIDS.

HAPPY: I'm …

ASPERA: I'm not Jewish but I am a dyke and I think, either way, AIDS equals Hebrew or the reverse, you're in BIG trouble. I'm going to beat you up.

HAPPY: Not *equals*, I … I'm lonely. I'm among playwrights. Back East for the first time in months. So I get to talk. And none of you listen anyway. In Culver City everyone listens, they listen listen listen. They take notes. They take you at your word. You are playwrights. So be inattentive. If you paid attention you'd be novelists.

FLATTY: Aspera has spent five years in London. She's acquired the listening disease.

OTTOLINE: Soon, unless she watches herself, she will be an American playwright no longer but British, her plays will be all nuance, inference.

FLATTY: Yes, nuance, unless she's careful, or a socialist feminist.

BIFF: Everyone hates you Flatty.

OTTOLINE: Oops.

FLATTY: [*Unphased, not missing a beat.*] And then there will be no nuance at all.

ASPERA: *Does* everyone hate you?

FLATTY: No, they don't.

ASPERA: I live in London now, I'm out of the loop.

FLATTY: They don't hate me, they envy me my money.

ASPERA: [*To* HAPPY.] I wouldn't *really* beat you up.

FLATTY: I could buy and sell the lot of you. Even *you* Happy and *you write sitcoms*. There. I've said it. I am wealthy. My plays have made me wealthy. I am richer than essayists, novelists, at least the respectable ones, and all poets ever. Envy is rather *like* hatred but as it's more debilitating to its votaries and votaresses [because it's so inherently undignified] it's of less danger ultimately to its targets.

BIFF: I don't envy your money. I envy your reviews.

HAUTFLOTE: I think we should dig now and bury Ding. This ground is patrolled. The night doesn't last forever. Ding's waiting.

OTTOLINE: [*Softly, firmly.*] Ding's dead.

I love this place. It was worth two hundred and thirty-seven dollars and fifty cents to get here. Yes Flatty you can pay my way. Send me a check. Biff's got a point. It's the reviews, isn't it. I've worked tirelessly for decades. Three at least. What I have done no one has ever done and no one does it nearly so well. But what I do is break the vessels because they never fit me right and I despise their elegance and I like the sound the breaking makes, it's a new music. What I do is make mess apparent or make apparent messes, I cannot tell which myself. I signal disenfranchisement, dysfunction, disinheritance well I *am* a black woman what do they expect it's hard stuff but it's life but I am *perverse* I do not want my stories straight up the narrative the narrative the miserable fucking narrative the universe is post-Cartesian post-Einsteinian it's not at any rate what it's post-to-be let's throw some curve balls already who cares if they never cross the plate it's hard too hard for folks to apprehend easy so I get no big money reviews and no box office and I'm broke, I'm fifty or sixty or maybe I've turned eighty, I collected the box at the Cafe Cinno yes I am THAT old, and poor but no matter, I have a great talent for poverty. Oblivion, on the other hand, scares me. Death. And this may shock you but [*To* FLATTY.] I ENVY you ... your RENOWN. [*Roaring.*] *I DON'T WANT ANOTHER OBIE! I want a hit! I want to hit a home run! I WANT A MARQUEE!* I'm too old to be ashamed of my hunger.

BIFF: O come to me short sweet. [*He blows a raspberry.*] There's just no dignity. I am oppressed by theater critics.

FLATTY: I gave up on dignity *years* ago. I am prolific. That's my revenge. If you want dignity you should marry a lighting designer.

OTTOLINE: Perhaps now we have worn out our terror, or at least winded it.

HAUTFLOTE: At darkest midnight December in the bleak mid-winter athwart the crest of Abel's Hill on Martha's Vineyard six moderately inebriated playwrights stood shovels poised to inter ...

FLATTY: Illegally.

HAUTFLOTE: ... the earthly remains of a seventh.

HAPPY: Who might at least have agreed to the convenience of a cremation.

HAUTFLOTE: Being a creature of paper as well as of the fleeting moment Ding naturally had a horror of fire. *I knew him best.* For a long time now. I loved him.

OTTOLINE: We all did.

HAUTFLOTE: Yet not one of us dares break ground.

HAPPY: Wind perhaps, but never ground.

ASPERA: Wind for sure but not the Law. But is it the law or what's underground which immobilizes us? Incarceration or an excess of freedom? Enchainment or liberation? For who knows what dreams may come? Who knows what's underneath? Who knows if anything is, if the shovel will strike stone, or pay dirt, or nothing whatsoever?

BIFF: It's the Nothing stopping me. I can speak only for myself.

FLATTY: Bad thing in a playwright.

BIFF: The horseleech hath two daughters. There's a play in there, somewhere, of course. I used to say: it won't come out. Fecal or something, expulsive metaphor. I was stuffed, full and withholding. In more generous times. Before the fear ... of the Deficit, before the Balanced Budget became the final face of the Angel of the Apocalypse. Now instead I say: I'm not going to go there. A geographical metaphor. Why? *I'm nearly forty* is one explanation. *"There"* meaning ... That bleachy bone land. Into that pit. That plot. To meet that deadline.

OTTOLINE: The play is due?

BIFF: Day after yesterday.

HAPPY: Rehearsals starting ... ?

BIFF: Start*ed*.

ASPERA: What, without a script?

BIFF: They're *improvising*.

[*Everyone shudders.*]

FLATTY: You shouldn't be here! You should be home writing!

BIFF: Did I mention how much I hate you, Flatty.

FLATTY: Marry a lighting designer. It worked for me. Sobered me right up.

HAPPY: I never meant ... This reverse transcription thing. I'll work on it.

ASPERA: You do that.

HAPPY: I never meant to equate Hebrew and ... It's just the words: reverse transcription. *Thinking* about it. Something I can't help doing. Writing began with the effort to record speech. All writing is an attempt to fix intangibles — thought, speech, what the eye observes — fixed on clay tablets, in stone, on paper. Writers *capture*. We playwrights on the other hand write or rather "wright" to set these free again. Not inscribing, not *de*-scribing but ... *ex*-scribing [?] ... "W-R-I-G-H-T," that archaism, because it's something earlier we do, cruder, something one does with one's mitts, one's paws. To claw words up ...!

[HAPPY *falls to his knees beside* DING *and starts to dig with his hands.*]

HAPPY: To startle words back into the air again, to ... evanesce. It is ... unwriting, to do it is to die; yes, but. A lively form of doom.

ASPERA: Ah, so now you are equating …

BIFF: It's not about *equation.* It's about the transmutation of horror into meaning.

ASPERA: Doomed to fail.

HAPPY: Dirty work … [*He shows his hands.*]

ASPERA: A mongrel business. This Un-earthing.

HAUTFLOTE: For which we Un-earthly are singularly fit. Now or never.

BIFF: I'm nearly forty. My back hurts.

FLATTY: Whose doesn't? No dignity but in our labors.

[*They hoist their shovels.*]

ASPERA: Goodnight old Ding. Rest easy baby. And flights of self-dramatizing hypochondriacal hypersensitive self-pitying paroxysmical angels saddlebag you off to sleep.

BIFF: [*Apostrophizing* DING'*s corpse.*] Oh Dog Weary.

HAUTFLOTE: Many of these graves are cenotaphs, you know, empty tombs, honorifics. Sailors lost on whalers, lost at sea, no body ever found, air and memory interred instead. All other headstones in the graveyard peristalithic to these few empty tombs, whose ghostly drama utterly overwhelms The Real.

[HAUTFLOTE *waves his hand in the air, a downbeat. Ella sings "When They Begin The Beguine."*]

OTTOLINE: Dig. Shovel tips to earth.

[*They are.*]

OTTOLINE: The smell of earth will rise to meet us. Our nostrils fill with dark brown, roots ends, decomposing warmth and man-ufactory, earthworm action. The loam.

FLATTY: I don't want to go to jail. Doesn't David Mamet live around here somewhere?

OTTOLINE: Push in.

[*They do.*]

THE END

David Mamet

THE JADE MOUNTAIN

David Mamet

David Mamet is the author of the plays *Oleanna, Glengarry Glen Ross* (1984 Pulitzer Prize and New York Drama Critics Circle Award), *American Buffalo, The Old Neighborhood, A Life In The Theater, Speed The Plow, Edmond, Lakeboat, The Water Engine, The Woods, Sexual Perversity In Chicago, Reunion* and *The Cryptogram* (1995 Obie Award). His translations and adaptations include *Red River* by Pierre Laville and *The Cherry Orchard, Three Sisters* and *Uncle Vanya* by Anton Chekhov. His films include *The Postman Always Rings Twice, The Verdict, The Untouchables, House Of Games* (writer/director), *Oleanna* (writer/director), *Homicide* (writer/director), *The Spanish Prisoner* (writer/director), *Hoffa, The Edge,* and *Wag The Dog.* Mr. Mamet is also the author of *Warm And Cold,* a book for children with drawings by Donald Sultan, and two other children's books, *Passover* and *The Duck And The Goat; Writing In Restaurants, Some Freaks,* and *Make-Believe Town,* three volumes of essays; *The Hero Pony,* a book of poems; *Three Children's Plays, On Directing Film, The Cabin,* and the novel *The Village.* His most recent books include a new novel, *The Old Religion,* and an acting book, *True & False.*

Two Men.

A: When the monkeys come up. But we didn't know what they were. We thought we were under attack. On the next day when it cleared, we were above the clouds. Most of the time. But it cleared, we were above the clouds. Most of the time. But it socked in, and when it cleared, back in Wisconsin, often you would wait, sometimes into the afternoon, 'til it burned off, but usually by ten or nine or by eleven anyway, one time I doused this balsa wood airplane. With lighter fluid, and put a string on it, and lighted the string. And threw it. By the Lake. And I felt guilty for it. Do you know, though I do not know why, unless it was that I was plain' with *fire;* yes, I think that is what it is, but the *curious* thing is that I should feel *guilty,* you know, when it never did ignite.

B: It didn't catch?

A: No.

B: The plane.

A: No. It didn't.

B: Did you soak the string?

A: The string.

B: The lighter fluid?

A: As I *spoke* I thought that you were gone' to ask me. And my first thought was "of course," but, as I think on it, I think how could I have, as it did not ignite, and subsequently, perhaps, that was the cause of my — it's not astonishment — of my *surprise* when it didn't catch.

B: Could the wind have blown it out?

A: ... but up above the clouds. [*Pause.*] Also. On our Observation Post. There was a *cave*, and it was naturally occurring. As I b'lieve they are. You hear "a manmade cave" ... you hear "A natural cave" ... which is it that you hear?

B: "A natural cave."

A: Yes. And "A manmade cave." But I think that you hear "a natural cave." When, *why* would you hear that, as I think *all* caves are natural? I was going to say, "All caves are natural except those that're *man*made." But I think you hear "a natural cave," and I think *all* caves are natural, for, if not, what are they? But holes in the earth. In a "hill," I suppose. They would have to be, and it *is* possible the wind blew it out; but, if so, then we're back to that same question of if I had gone and soaked it in the gasoline, and, if not, *why* not. For could I not of known that if I did *not* the wind would blow it out, and further, perhaps I *desired* that the plane would not catch, what do you think; and *if* that is the case, that I *contrived* it not to burn, then why would I feel guilty?

You could look back and say "what a child — to have devised a scheme to *be* and *not* be that thing which he wished both to be and not to be."

B: And what was that?

A: I want to say "a mischief maker," but I think that's not the thing.

B: What is the thing? [*Pause.*] What is the thing, then?

A: A man.

B: He wished to be a man.

A: I think that is what it is, and I still haven't told you about the Etruscan Statue. In *breaking* a thing, a rule, a way-of-being, perhaps.

B: To become a man. By doing that.

A: I think so. But then why would I feel guilty? Anyways. We thought that we were under attack. And we heard this *chattering*. [*Pause.*] Humans talking. Humans talking. Why would they, why would they *talk* so loud, you'd say, if they were trying to avoid detection. I don't know. Do you know, several times in my life. I have heard ghosts. And it's a common story. In Wisconsin. Up near the Northern Peninsula. In the North. I think there's something fitting about that. Do you?

B: I don't know.

A: And it seems there is and I think there are plots of land. Which exude things. [*Pause.*] I don't think that we create them there. I think they *live* there. I think they live there. There were ghosts. Several times. I could describe them to you.

B: What were they?

A: Well, they were noises. On the edge of sleep, you'd hear them. Or reading a book. When your thoughts ...

B: ... when your thoughts were elsewhere.

A: That's right. People talking. Talking low. "What is that out there?" Seldom when there was anyone there. In the trailer. Who you could say. Who you could look to, not even for, for *comfort*.

B: What is wrong with comfort?

A: ... but, later, to say, "Wasn't that real? What *was* that? That 'talking'." There was no one there. There was nobody there. How could there have been? In the woods. And what would they, why had they come there. In the middle of the night?

B: To do you harm.

A: I can't say so. Then why was I frightened? Do you know? And *at the time.* [*Pause.*] Once I took a gun to see. I started out the door. As I went out the door, I said, "I do not want to know." And, I'll tell you: I said to myself at the time, "Are you *content.* To spend the rest of your life *knowing* that you lacked the strength. To go out that door." And I said, if the test is to go out that door, or to stay, then I am going to stay.

B: And are you content?

A: No. I never was content.

[*Pause.*]

B: Would you like a cup of tea?

A: Yes. I would.

[B *gestures off.*]

B: Are you tired?

A: Yes. I am. What is contentment, *finally*, I don't know, but *'enough'*, when you have been deprived, perhaps, do you think?

B: I don't know.

A: But that could be one of the definitions.

B: Yes. Certainly.

A: Couldn't it?

B: Yes. It could.

A: When I looked at the *rock*. [*Pause.*] I had pictures of it somewhere. Where have they gone? Funny, that the things which mean something to *me*, what can they mean to *you*? Finally. What can they mean. Nothing, really. Things that happened. If I told you. Once in a museum. Six men. Schemed for a week. To remove a priceless artifact. Beyond price. And what happened to it. Or the mountain. Things that made us. What we are. After all the shit of this world. And all philosophy. And thought. And religion. And literature. What makes us, then, but a rest. When we are tired, or warmth. When we are cold. A release of some sort. Friendship, maybe, then, is just we know that they aren't going to kill us. But we had to go through it. *Don't* we? Can you *doubt* it? To come out again? [*Pause.*] Then why do I feel so guilty ...

[C *brings in tea things and departs.*]

... over it? But when they tried to hit the rock they could not hit it. We had *no* ricochets in the cave. *No* rounds. *Nothing*. All of it outside. [*Pause.*] Outside. On the rock. And we *lay* on it. And peppered the trail. At will. For it ran into China. And if we found them on it, they were either going *in* or coming *out*. Either way. Well, good. They're gonna play "catch up"? Now, I can't blame 'em. But you aren't going to get *in* there. I think someone took 'em on the Hospital Ship. Do you know, you never meet a guy but that some buddy, or hear "heard" of someone won two hundred thousand dollars coming back, a poker game, a crap game, something — but I do not think it's true. Do you see, those are the *true* stories of the Supernatural. [*Of tea.*] There's nothing in this.

B: What do you mean?

[*Pause.*]

A: There's nothing in this.

B: Of what sort? Is that a question? [*Pause.*] What would there be in it? [*Pause.*] In the cup. Do you mean?

A: Perhaps if I drank it I'd have a dream. Did you ever think that? That you would be released, or that you been poisoned? Many thought that.

B: ... they did ...

A: Yes. That someone had *adulterated* a drink. And it never was *food*, do you know? But a drink. And it made them crazy.

B: ... that someone had put something in their drink.

A: But I said coffee itself was sufficient.

B: To?

A: To *warp* you. To speed you up. So *thoroughly* you never would come home. Let alone ... [*Sighs.*] And, in Olden Days. I would blow half a pack of Camels in the last ten miles of a march. Meant *nothing* to me. On Deck. On the Med cruise, bet against our man, did fifteen hundred pushups, perhaps. I *myself* did five, six hundred. It was *nothing*. And the coffee, I think, burned, or irritated me. Or something. To the point I had grown old. And I can't do it. [*Pause.*] No. I can't do it. The foods that I ate. The deeds I did. [*Pause.*] "Behave appropriately, then." you might say. But I don't know. It's a shithole. Isn't it?

Praying for some, some, something to lift, then, you say, "I'm happy now." When you remember *life* was when you didn't think about it, and that's all it was.

B: But isn't that a part of?

A: Fuck you, then. Were you *there?* You cannot *begin* to imagine. What we did. Where we *were* … what we *did* … For I tell you. [*Pause.*] A mountain made of Jade. Carved figures. Hewn from it. Of the *Buddha* … and, acrost, of the Blessed Virgin, and such Gold, that if we took one chalice. Or bowl, each of us, would be beyond, *beyond* fabulous wealth. *Beyond, beyond* the Etruscan Statue. Encrusted with Jewels. As they lay there. [*Pause.*] But we took nothing.

The essence of it was the Guard. But if he was so ineffective could that be his people, you see, this is what concerned me, in the time that past, had wanted to invite rather than to dissuade us. From going in.

B: I believe we have to move on.

A: Also, could you not, however, say the same of any temptation?

B: Of course you could.

A: Someone said "the vase will free us." I don't think so. For how many times were we not possessed of that thing we thought was the talisman, only to have it shatter, some sort? That guy on the deck. When the ship was "et up" with our bloke did the fifteen hundred, and they welshed on up, the vase, that dropped off his lap, getting from the car. The one round that entered that cave. On the Hospital Ship. Some guy, Huh. *You* wouldn't know him. His spine severed. Shit, you say, I'd rather be screaming than drugged. But that's not the case — and at the *end* I must say that the voices were those I would wrong. In later life, for I can not, for the *life* of me, give you another reading of who in the world they could be. And what they were striving to tell me. [*Pause.*] *Why* did the plane not burn?

B: The point not that it did not burn, but you were guilty as you did not wish it to.

A: Is that the case? Is that the thing of it, then? Is that what you came to tell me? [*Pause.*] Well. [*Pause.*] Well, that's not nothing. [*Pause.*] And if they *had* transpired, then we would not be here today. Isn't that true?

[*Pause.*]

B: Yes. That's true.

A: And we have to move on ...

B: Yes.

A: Well, then. [*Pause.*] Well, then. [*Pause.*] Then, let's do that, then.

END OF PLAY

John Ford Noonan

WHAT DROVE ME BACK TO RECONSIDERING MY FATHER

This play is dedicated to Jennifer Kellow and Bridget McCart, with special thanks to Lorraine Brennan.

John Ford Noonan

John Ford Noonan is a 1989 inductee into the French Society of Composers and Authors. He first came to prominence in 1969 with the highly acclaimed Lincoln Center production of *The Year Boston Won the Pennant*, starring Roy Scheider. It won Noonan an Obie, a Theatre World and a Pulitzer nomination.

From 1972 to 1977 at Joe Papp's New York Shakespeare Festival, Noonan wrote *Older People* (a Drama Desk Award Winner), *Concerning the Effects of Trimethylchloride*, *Where Do We Go From Here?*, *All the Sad Protestants*, and *Getting Through the Night*. In 1978 his play *The Club Champion's Widow*, with Maureen Stapleton, opened the premiere season of the Robert Lewis Acting Company.

In the 1980's he wrote *A Coupla White Chicks Sitting Around Talking*, which ran for more than 800 performances at the Astor Place Theatre, and *Some Men Need Help* (three months on Broadway). In 1987 Mr. Noonan's *Spanish Confusion*, *Mom Sells Twins for Two Beers*, *Green Mountain Fever*, and *Recent Developments In Southern Connecticut* all ran simultaneously in Los Angeles (three of which won Drama-Logue Awards). In 1990, Mr. Noonan wrote his play *Talking Things Over With Chekhov* and also performed the male lead for six months at the Actor's Playhouse. In 1993, the WPA presented his play *Music From Down the Hill*. It was subsequently produced, under the direction of Dorothy Lyman, at the Odyssey Theatre in Los Angeles.

Noonan has twice been annointed for an Emmy — in 1984 for an episode of *St. Elsewhere* called "The Women" (which he won) and in 1985 for the television adaptation of *Some Men Need Help*. On screen he has acted in such movies as *Brown Wolf*; *Next Stop, Greenwich Village*; *Heaven Help Us*; *Adventures in Babysitting*, and in the hit movie *Flirting With Disaster*.

Mr. Noonan's proudest accomplishments to date are 1) his children: Jesse Sage Noonan, Chris Noonan Howell, Olivia Noonan Howell, and Tracy Noonan Howell, and his secret and favorite fifth, Tom Noonan Nohilly; 2) his acclaim by *Rolling Stone* magazine as "the greatest white boogie dancer in the world"; 3) his being founding member of the legendary punk band "Pinhead," as well as penning their anthem, "Kill Your Parents, Then We'll Talk"; 4) his being four consecutive times Junior Golf Champion at his home country club in Greenwich, CT. He once shot a sixty-seven followed by an eighty-one and 5) he loves sentences. His utter favorite utterance in his whole life was his mother's recent remark, "John, it's never too late to be normal."

TIME: *Late April. Wednesday. Balmy breeze, NYC spring day. Just after 4 P.M.*

PLACE: *201 West 58th Street. 9th floor, Apt. 9-B. A bedroom in a large seven-room apartment that has been rented from an old friend.* DANA *has done everything possible to make it her own. Simple but tasteful furniture, large bookcase filled with books, couch that converts to queen-size bed. Center of room table with phone on it. Next to phone* PLAY SCRIPT OF ONE ACT MONOLOGUE ...

Lights up! DANA *pours large double Scotch over ice at bar area in bookcase. Turns and serves Scotch to "DOLL" of her* FATHER, *sitting at table [Doll is 2/3's lifesize, incredibly accurate face.]* ... LONG SILENCE ...

DANA: You've looked at your liquor the same way ever since I was six years old.

[*Pause.*]

Just letting it sit there ... like "THE LONGER YOU WAIT, THE BETTER IT'LL GET."

[*Pause.*]

So there I'd be, sitting on your lap, and after a long time looking you'd suddenly guzzle it down and then gagging like a deep sea diver desperate for air, you'd gasp out ... how was it you'd gasp out? ... Oh yeah!

[*Imitating* "FATHER" *gasping out.*]

"DADDY NEEDS SOME MORE OIL AND ICE." I'd jump

up, go and get the bottle, back then it was bourbon, and load you back up. Then you'd start all over with the looking and the holding back, ... Then, ... then once more the guzzling and gagging.

[*Laughing in fond memory.*]

By the time you'd have four or five you'd get that far away look. Suddenly I wasn't your six year old anymore but some magical, mysterious princess and we'd sing one of those songs you loved.

[DANA *breaks into a lovely version of Someone To Watch Over Me.*]

With that done, you'd bark out like some crazed pagan honcho.

[*Again "imitating"* FATHER.]

"ONE LAST OIL FOR THE LAST BIG HILL!" One last time I'd load you up and we'd start off to bed singing only by now we'd be mostly humming ... and I was becoming your "JUNE BRIDE!!"

[*Again "imitating"* FATHER.]

"WOULD MY JUNE BRIDE LIKE A RIDE UPSTAIRS?" And you'd carry me to my bedroom and tuck me in only cause you were so oiled lots of times you'd fall asleep next to me ...

[*Imitating* "MOTHER".] "I WON'T HAVE THIS IN MY HOUSE!!"

Boy, did that make Mom nuts.

Finding us asleep.

[*Laughing.*]

She's dead. We're not. Drink up!! Come on, "ONE LAST OIL FOR THE LAST BIG HILL."

[*Pause. Suddenly* DANA *seems at a loss for words. Checks "play script" next to phone, discovers where she is, continues to* DOLL.]

Remember that play we made up. It was called ... it was called ... oh, yeah!! *JUNE BRIDE AND KING BIG BELLY.*

It was the first time you made a whole lot of money so I was suddenly in private school where all the other kids called me "awesome" cause I had my city public licks down so totally.

[*Imitating "SELF".*]

"FAR FUCKING OUT! ANYTHING FAB ON THE SCOPE?" That's one of my favorite sections. Why do I want to keep leaving it out?

[*Puts script down. Picks up Scotch, returns to bar area,* "MIMES" *refilling drink and returning to table and* FATHER *starts scene again all the way from the beginning.*]

"YOU'VE LOOKED AT YOUR LIQUOR THE SAME WAY EVER SINCE I WAS SIX YEARS OLD."

[*Pause.*]

"JUST LETTING IT SIT THERE ..."

[*Suddenly* PHONE *rings.* DANA *momentarily shocked but picks up receiver and answers call.*]

Hello? ... Yes, this is Felice Perlman. Actually for a year and some eleven weeks I've been Dana Renwick but before that yes I went by Felice Perlman ... Excuse me but may I ask who's calling?

[*Pause.*]

Hello? ... Hello? ... Hello? ...

[*Hangs phone back up. Again starts scene all the way from the beginning.*]

"YOU'VE LOOKED AT YOUR LIQUOR THE SAME WAY EVER SINCE I WAS SIX YEARS OLD."

[*Pause.*]

"JUST LETTING IT SIT THERE."

[*Stops, grabs up script, races toward a later section, checks dialogue, puts down script, resumes talking to doll of* FATHER.]

I'm telling you I waited on you that day. No, no, I was your waitress but you never even ...

[*Suddenly laughing.*]

She was ... oh, 27, 28, blonde, built, lovely green eyes and a beauty mark like Madonna only on the left ... No, no, you ordered a double Johnny Walker Black neat with a soda back and she had a tequilla sunrise with extra ice on the side ... Daddy, I wasn't doing one of my crazy accents, just good old overweight me. I know I've gained a lot since the last time but not to recognize your own goddamn daughter is pretty ...

[*Pause.*]

O.K., I'm a few feet from your table with the sunrise and the JW Black when suddenly you reach across, take her hand, and beg, "JUST CAUSE HE'S YOUNGER DOESN'T MEAN HE'S BETTER." ... No, no, lots of times when Mom was dying I'd hear you turn on the sincere

[*"Imitating"* FATHER.]

"DON'T TALK LIKE THAT. MY KIDDO'S GOING TO OUT LAST BOTH OF US, FELICE, RIGHT?"

[*Pause.*]

Oh how about?!!

[*Again "imitating"* FATHER.]

"NOW THAT IT'S CRUNCH CITY, I'M HERE FOR MY BABY DAY AND NIGHT. KIDDO, I LOVE YOU."

[*Pause.*]

No, no, sincere I'd seen. What I'd never seen in my whole life was you need something so bad and be able to talk about it without lying!!

[*Again "imitating"* FATHER.]

"JUST CAUSE HE'S YOUNGER DOESN'T MEAN HE'S BETTER" certainly doesn't sound deep, memorable, or anything much but coming from you — well, I ran back to the bar and this day bartender Patty Hart — no, no but he's the first man I've ever felt completely open with — anyway, Patty says

[*Imitating "PATTY HART".*]

"WHAT'S UP, HUSKY?" ... and I just ...

[*Suddenly* PHONE *rings.* DANA *smiles as though she knows who it is. Casually lifts receiver and casually talks into it.*]

Hi, Dad ... Sure been a while, hasn't it though?!!

[*Laughing.*]

Cause you always have someone call ahead to make sure the ... Yes, but when they asked for Felice Perlmen, then I absolutely ... Dad, last Christmas I wrote you and ...

[*Suddenly stopping.*]

Sure, Dad, but don't take too long

[*While she waits, she gives violent slap to* DOLL'*s face.* FATHER *returns on other end.*]

Good ... Last Christmas I wrote you a very long and elaborate note. I explained how I was changing my name because something told me Dana Renwick was much more ... yes, yes, but it's just like you to receive a long and impassioned request and then six months later totally disregard it. Dad, right now, say "HI, DANA RENWICK" ... But ... Of course I'm still ...

[*Suddenly stopping.*]

Yes, yes, I'll hold on ... only ...

[*While she waits, she gives another violent slap to* DOLL'*s face. Again,* FATHER *returns.*]

Good ... Anyway, that's how come I knew it was you when I picked up the phone!

[*Pause.*]

Actually, Dad, it's been 5 years, 7 months, and 13 days since we talk-ed ... except of course with the doll of you here that I'm continually ...

[*Laughing.*]

Just a little joke, ha, ha, ha!

[*Pause.*]

No, no. When I called your secretary Monday she said it might be a week to ten days cause you were in Madrid on business ... so the fact that it's only been three days makes me feel sort of half daughterly, ha, ha, ha! ... No, no, it's just that ...

[*Pause.*]

You say you came back early cause you had a hunch it was super important ...

[*Laughing, suddenly stops.*]

Don't lie, Daddy. Please not today.

[*Exploding.*]

Cause you were never away! Cause you were in your office every day this week!! Dad, yesterday, Tuesday right around the corner from your office you had lunch at O'Neal's on 57th and 6th with the same young girl you always ...

[*Pause.*]

The day bartender Patty Hart told me. It was my day off ... Right, Mondays and Tuesdays! Dad, I've been a waitress there almost a year. I've stood in the window on Fridays when you always leave work a little early ... always between 3:45 and 4, right? ... I've watched you hail a cab! Daddy, a month ago I saw you knock down a guy about 30 who tried to steal ... I know punching power is the last to go. I've been hearing it since I was six years old. I know ... yes but ...

[*Exploding.*]

We could go on and on but just tell me why you lied about being in Spain. I can forgive anything but the lying has always ...

[*Pause.*]

Dad, 5 years, 7 months and 13 days ago I was playing one of the leads in that John Ford Noonan play. Right, only ... Dad, if you don't let me talk, it's going to be another five years!

[*Pause.*]

You were in the audience that night. It was our fourth preview. A small house. 31 people. You were in the third row, ticket C-7 ... Three times you howled uncontrollably. Seven times you slapped your knees. Every time I did something funny your laughter kissed me with approval. Once you were so loud the woman ahead in B-5 had to "SHUSH" you. Afterwards we went out. That nice restaurant you always

[*Screaming.*]

Who cares who picked up the check! ... When I got there, you and Noonan were already ordering your second drinks. Noonan jumped up and hugged me. You stared at your drink as you've stared at every drink since I was six years old. I sat down. You looked up and said "NOONAN'S NO SLOUCH. DAMN INTERESTING. FIRST RATE SECOND ACT." I reach across, take your hand. "DADDY, WHAT DID YOU THINK OF YOUR DAUGHTER?" You guzzle your drink and say "FOR ALL YOUR INEXPERIENCE, NOT HALF BAD" ... No, no, that's not what ... Shut your mouth, O.K.! ... "FOR ALL YOUR EXPERIENCE, NOT HALF BAD" Dad, I was brilliant, great, and amazing that night ... but mostly because your laughter fed me, drove me on. We had helped each other, been one and ...

[*Exploding.*]

Dad, you lied to me that night. You lied to me this morning. Lying's killed us all the way back to when I was little and you'd never quite come clean. Dad, don't try and ...
[*Pause.*]
Daddy, no, no. You were continually in stitches. Three times you howled uncontrollably. Seven times you slapped your knees. Every time I did something funny, your laughter ...

[*Laughing.*]

Because my friend sitting next to you in C-5, my friend CASEY ST. JOHN, well, he recorded everything you did. Your laughs, chuckles, twice you said "CASEY, ISN'T MY BABY SOMETHING ELSE?"

[*Pause.*]

I still listen to it. I've edited it down to the highlights but ... About six weeks ago I did because there's this play I've written that's about you and me only ...

[*Pause.*]

Could you please ask them to call back? There's this incredibly important thing I'm about to say! ... No, no, it won't take more than ...

[*Pause.*]

If you hang up now, don't ever call back. O.K., now. What I'm so excited about is that in this one-act I've ...

[*Pause*]

Hello? ... Hello? ... Hello? ...

[DANA *hangs up phone. Crosses to cabinet, takes out small cassette recorder and puts on table by phone. Next she gets cassette tape out of box, returns to table, sits down, puts tape in recorder and listens. It is the edited highlights of her father watching her act: the uncontrollable howling. The laughter, twice we hear him say "CASEY, ISN'T MY BABY SOMETHING ELSE." Last thing we hear is his excitement when audience cheers* DAUGHTER's *curtain call. At end he says "OH GOD, OH GOD." Suddenly phone rings.* DANA *picks it up and talks into receiver.*]

It's been a long time since you surprised me, Daddy. The last time was, right, my graduation when you ... right ... God, was that funny, funny, funny!!

[DANA *begins to laugh, starts to cry, fights it off, back to laughter ... Then quiet breathing.*]

No, no! Daddy, I've got this present to share with you. Promise you'll just listen and not interrupt ...

[*Puts down receiver, picks up one-act play script, races through it in search of which section to read* FATHER *first. Throws script down, back into receiver.*]

You still there? ... Oh, WOW!!

[*Nervously laughing.*]

I'm not going to read from the play. I'm going to just tell it.

[*Nervous.*]

Dad, I've gained almost thirty pounds since the night of the Noonan play. I know, I know, I used to be your "WHISPEY WONDER" but now I'm your "CHUNKY HUNK."

[*Laughing.*]

I'm sorry to laugh at my jokes but somehow these past few years have been a time when I needed some real meat on my bones. It made me feel solid and safe, sorta like Uncle Phil. But ...

[*Pause.*]

Dad, why don't you wait till you see me. Lots of people think I'm better looking.

[*Yelling.*]

Daddy, fat or thin I'm the only non-beauty in your life so ... so why don't we just ... Anything you say will be a lie so ... Dad, DON'T.

[*Rage erupting.*]

Your only kid ain't good enough looking for her dad to even ask out on a date, Amen, end of how I look for-goddamn-ever.

[*Pause.*]

Anyway, a little over a year ago I was walking north up Sixth Avenue. Head down, a pint of Haagen Dazs chocolate-chocolate chip in one hand, plastic spoon in the other, I come upon *O'NEAL'S* at the corner of 57th and 6th. I finish my chocolate-chocolate chip and say to the manager when he walks up to me at the door, "WOULD YOU CONSIDER A LADY WHO NEEDS TO DO A GOOD JOB?" He barks back, "FAT O.K. BUT ARE YOU FAST?" He lets me try out on this station near the bar that no one has been able to conquer. Difficult regulars, mid-day drunks, impatient out-of-towners. The other waitresses call my station "DEATH VALLEY." Dad, I'm an instant hit in "DEATH VALLEY." Everyone talks to me — customers, fellow workers, hitters at the bar.

[*Laughing wildly.*]

I know I'm almost 40 with nothing but a coupla show case plays to show for it but for the first time in my life there's some place that I want to be at on time. Anyway, one day some time last summer I'm serving one of my mid-day drunks his fourth Jack Daniels on the rocks when I look up and Roz Cash is sitting you by the window on station four. Dad, you looked as handsome as ever. To think that at 65 ... O.K., 64 you still look so great, well ... anyway, I said nothing. Went back to work. As you left, I ask Roz Cash "WHO'S THE GREY HAIRED DUDE IN THE CARDIN SUIT?" "AARON PERLMAN, A REGULAR," Roz purrs back. Oh God, I'll be seeing you, running into you regularly. But no, you never show again. September, October, early November, no sign of Daddy. The Tuesday before Thanksgiving about six months ago, I see you out the window hailing a cab. I race out "DADDY, DADDY,

WHERE HAVE YOU BEEN?" ... only it's not you. Christmas, New Year's, that awful week of snow in early February, I begin to worry. Patty Hart, my best friend day bartend-er ... no, no, that's all, friends ... he calls your office and they say you're in London till March. March comes and goes, the first week of April, the second, I'm panicked. Patty comforts me with this real Irish, "IT WON'T BE LONG NOW, HUSKY." It wasn't. April 15th, 3:55 P.M. a Wednesday I see you out the window punch out a guy half your age who's trying to steal your ...

[*Pause.*]

Have I already told you that? ... Oh yeah!! Right!!! I thought I only told the doll in the play. Anyway, the day following April 20th, 12:15, in you walk with her. Roz Cash sits you at Sharon's station by the window but it's all been worked out by my beloved Patty Hart. I quietly switch with Sharon, walk up to you — you're already fondling her hand all lovey-dovey — and I say "ANYTHING FROM THE BAR TO START EITHER OF YOU OUT?"

[*Laughing.*]

Yes, Daddy, I waited on you but you didn't know it was me. Oh, re-ally? ... You ordered a double Johnny Walker neat with a soda back and she had a tequilla sunrise with extra ice on the side.

[*Pause.*]

No, no, Daddy, she was very pretty. Those green eyes were about the most ... and that build, WOW!! ... So what if you're forty years older. If you two are meant ...

[*Laughing.*]

O.K., so I'm on my way back to you with your drinks, five or six feet away, no more and suddenly there's someone new at the table — I mean it's you, Dad — please shut up, O.K. — No, no, just a you with an expression I'd never known. Tears coming down your cheeks, well, I'd never ... As I put the two drinks down, you suddenly grabbed her hand and blurt out, "JUST CAUSE HE'S YOUNGER DOESN'T MEAN HE'S BETTER!!" She pulls her hand away. You guzzle your drink "REFILL, HONEY, PLEASE MAKE IT QUICK!" I race over to Patty and return with your refill just as you whisper "GIVE ME ONE MORE CHANCE. SEE IF I CAN CHANGE." I put your drink down. You grab my hand, stare me dead in the eye, "AM I THE SORT OF MAN YOU COULD TURN YOUR BACK ON?" I want to say "NO" but your girl darts in with — ... Daddy, you remember the sentence but not that it was me? Well, that's so you: remembering what you did but not who you did it to! Anyway, I recover my waitressness and counter with "WOULD THE LOVELY YOUNG LADY LIKE A REFILL AS WELL?" Green eyes says back "HE'S THE DRINKER. I'M THE SIPPER." You follow with "IF I ONLY SIP, WILL YOU STICK?" I smile, you smile but she doesn't get it. Her not getting it, I mean, I close my eyes hoping you'll see that her not getting it meant you two ...

[*Pause.*]

I know, Daddy, I know. Only instead of you getting her not getting it, your face suddenly got so red I thought you were going to explode ... yes, yes, something enormous inside you didn't know how to let out and that pointing to your heart, well, for a second I thought it was your ticker ... no, no, Daddy, it'll only be a few more ...

Stop it, NOW!!

[*Pause.*]

Dad, it was at that moment I saw that the pointing at your heart
was about all those feelings you'd never been able to find words
for ... No, no, you had all these incredible emotions with no gift
for the sentence that could set them free ... But, Dad ... Shut
up, O.K., and do me one favor: can you find words now for
what you couldn't say to her then? ... See what I'm saying!!
Even weeks after you're still so stuffed you —

[*Pause.*]

Dad, you are so ... no, no, it's so simple: you've got eighth grade
feelings but only first grade sentences, don't you see? But ...
Don't even breathe while I tell you my theory of sentences.
Ready? ... I have come to believe in sentences. That whatever
pain, fear, dread, rage you've got inside, there's a sentence
that goes with it. The sentence is like the key to the lock.
Once found, you put the sentence into the feeling and turn it
and SHAZAAM, out it comes.

[*Laughing.*]

Of course, it sounds a little crazy and often it doesn't always work
but look what it's goddamn led to!

[*Pause.*]

No, no, if you don't let me finish right now I'll ... Thanks.
Anyway, you and Green Eyes leave. I can't wait for my lunch
shift to be over. I race home. It's only a few hundred yards. 58th
and 7th, the northeast corner. I rent a bedroom with my own
bathroom. No, no I share that with a beautiful ex-model and
her beautiful 8 year old daughter who's already a model. Anyway,
the minute I get home the doll of you is sitting at my table!

[*Laughing.*]

Remember Noonan, right? Anyway, last year he wrote a play with a doll in it. He promised me I could have it as a present once the run was over. Yes, yes, and he left it while I was serving you lunch. It was still the body of the doll but Noonan had gotten his friend who built it to change the face so it looked like you. No, no I sit down and begin talking to the doll like it's you ... and then soon after the doll begins talking back. I mean, not really talking back but it's as if I hear this voice of you and so I copy it down ... No, no, on a piece of paper. I read it over and over. Suddenly I see it's a great way to end a play. I know, I know ... I've never written a play but somehow I can tell it's this great ending. These things the doll of you finally comes out with ... No, no, I'm not telling you the ending. You've got to see the whole thing.

[*Laughing.*]

Right, I've written a whole play about us. It's called *WHAT DROVE ME BACK TO RECONSIDERING MY FATHER*. In a lot of ways it's a lot like what we're trying to do right now ... only at the end the doll of you finally puts the key into his lock and ...

[*Laughing.*]

Yes, yes, it's a totally up ending. Anyway, on this Monday night there's a reading of it at Patrick O'Neal's loft down in the West 20's. 8:00 P.M. The address is 233 West 26th. He's the owner of the bar, right, but he does these Monday night readings and when Noonan showed him my play, well, ... that was it!!!

[*Pause.*]

Of course I'm not a real playwright yet but if this catches on, I'll try more and maybe then you'll call me one.

[*Pause.*]

You're right. I was being cynical but you made me feel like crap so why shouldn't I punch back. Dad, for years and years we've been putting needles in each other's eyes. We have been punching each other and pretending it was hugs. We've ...

[*Pause.*]

What do you mean "WOULD I LIKE TO GO OUT TO DINNER BEFORE?"!! Dad, are you trying to suggest that you'll be there on Monday night?

[*Laughing.*]

Dad, I can't go out before! Because I play myself in the play ... No, no, a wonderful actor by the name of Roy Scheider does the voice of you. Through a microphone hooked to the back of the doll's neck. Dad, please shut up!! We'll go out to dinner after, O.K.? ... No, no, I'm sure Noonan'd love to come. I'll bet you I can even get Roy Scheider!. He wants to meet you too! ... Oh, Daddy, tell me you're not lying. Tell me you're going to come.

[*Pause.*]

Say it again!

[*Pause.*]

Once more!!

[*Pause.*]

Dad, you're finally starting to get the key in the lock.

[*Laughing.*]

8:00 P.M. this coming Monday night, 233 West 26th, top floor! Dad, come alone, don't drink before and most of all bring your checkbook. I need 7,500 dollars to open my play in an equity showcase ... Right! Dad, this is even better than the way the play ends!! See you Monday night. Be ready to be proud.

[DANA *jumps up and down, runs around table, sits down, laughs, addresses* DOLL *across from her.*]

I've done it. I've done it. I've done it! Oh tell me I'm amazing, special and great.

DOLL: [*Suddenly speaking.*] SUPPOSE YOU ARE, BUT IT'S NOT.

[DANA *stunned, gets up and checks for microphone hooked to back of* DOLL'*s neck. Checks all around. Baffled. Confused.*]

DANA: You're not Roy Scheider.

DOLL: I SAID, "SUPPOSE YOU ARE, BUT IT'S NOT."

DANA: What's not?

DOLL: THE PLAY. SUPPOSE IT'S NOT AMAZING, SPECIAL AND GREAT? IT'S JUST OKAY?

DANA: I'll work on it. I'll rewrite it. I'll do it. I'll make it good.

DOLL: BUT WHAT IF IT DOESN'T TURN OUT THE WAY YOU DREAM IT?

DANA: This time I can do it.

DOLL: BABY, YOU'RE ALMOST 40 YEARS OLD.

DANA: I'll be 43 in October.

DOLL: PEOPLE AT 43 JUST DON'T SUDDENLY DO IT.

DANA: Daddy, please.

DOLL: I SEE IT EVERY MORNING ON MY WAY TO WORK. I CUT ACROSS 46TH STREET AND ALL THESE ACTORS ARE LINED UP IN FRONT OF THE EQUITY BUILDING. THEY'RE NOT GOING TO SUDDENLY DO IT. I SEE THE SAME THING IN THEIR EYES THAT I SEE IN YOURS: TERROR, FEAR AND HURT. YOU CAN'T JUST BE SOMETHING BECAUSE YOU WANT TO BE. IT'S GOT TO BURN IN YOU LIKE A HUGE, RAGING FLAME.

DANA: Daddy, look into my eyes. I have that flame now.

DOLL: BABY, I KNEW IT WAS YOU THE FIRST DAY YOU SERVED ME AND MY GIRLFRIEND AT O'NEALS. I HEARD YOUR VOICE. MY GIRLFRIEND SAID, "WHAT A BEAUTIFUL FACE. TOO BAD SHE CAN'T LOSE A FEW POUNDS."

DANA: Dad, please stop.

DOLL: BABY, FROM THE DAY YOU WERE 7 YEARS OLD, ALL YOU REALLY WANTED TO DO WAS FIT IN, BE ONE OF THE GIRLS, BE NORMAL AND ORDINARY.

[DANA *rips arm of* DOLL. DOLL *continues to talk.*]

OR WHAT ABOUT THE TIME WHEN YOU WERE 11 AND WE WORKED SO HARD AT HITTING AND CATCHING FLY BALLS SO THAT YOU COULD TRY OUT FOR LITTLE LEAGUE AND AT THE LAST MINUTE YOU GOT SICK AND DIDN'T WANT TO GO? OR THE TIME I WORKED WITH YOU ON YOUR CHEERLEADING MOVES IN JUNIOR HIGH, AND YOU DIDN'T EVEN MAKE THE FIRST CUT?

[DANA *rips off other arm of* DOLL. DOLL *continues to talk.*]

WHAT ABOUT ALL OF THOSE HOURS WE SPENT PREPARING FOR THE S.A.T? 537 MATH AND 490 ENGLISH ISN'T AMAZING, SPECIAL OR GREAT.

[DANA *slaps* DOLL *in face.* DOLL *continues to talk.*]

YOU LIVE IN THAT HORRIBLE VALLEY THAT ALMOST ALL PARENTS HAVE TO FACE IN THEIR CHILDREN. YOU'RE ABOVE AVERAGE, BUT YOU ARE NOT AMAZING, SPECIAL OR GREAT. YOU CAN NEVER GET UP THE MOUNTAIN TO GREATNESS, BUT YOU CAN'T GO BACK THE OTHER WAY AND BE NORMAL. IT BREAKS MY HEART THE WAY YOU ARE TRAPPED, BUT SOMEONE MUST FINALLY TELL YOU. DANA, OR WHATEVER YOU CALL YOURSELF, YOU ARE NOT SPECIAL, AMAZING AND GREAT, BUT I LOVE YOU AS MY DAUGHTER.

[DANA *sears head off of* DOLL, *but* DOLL *continues talking.*]

I HAVE NOT BEEN A PERFECT FATHER, BUT YOU HAVE NOT BEEN A PERFECT DAUGHTER. I DON'T WANT TO BE OLD AND IN A WHEELCHAIR AND RUN INTO YOU AT 60 YEARS OLD WOBBLING UP 6TH AVENUE EATING ICE CREAM. PLEASE STOP... STOP ... STOP ... STOP ... STOP ... STOP ...

[DANA *finally beats head of* DOLL *into submission. Pause. Cross to script on table. Picks it up and rips out final pages. Begins writing.*]

DANA: Now I know the real ending to the play.

END OF PLAY

Jules Tasca

DEUS-X

For Jay Brennan who worked on the world premiere.

Jules Tasca

Jules Tasca has taught playwriting at Oxford University in England and he has performed with a Commedia dell' arte group in Central Italy. He is the author of 105 (13 full length, 92 one-act) published plays that have been produced in numerous national theaters from The Mark Taper Forum to the Bucks County Playhouse, as well as abroad. He has also written for radio and television. He scripted "The Hal Linden T.V. Special." His *La Liorona* and *Maria* were produced on National Public Radio. Other one-act pieces were broadcast in Los Angeles and abroad in Germany. He was the national winner in New York's Performing Arts Repertory Theater playwriting contest for his libretto, *The Amazing Einstein*, which toured the country and played at the Kennedy Center in Washington, D.C. He has adapted the stories of Oscar Wilde, Guy de Maupassant, Mark Twain, Robert Louis Stevenson, Saki, and has modernized Aristophanes' *Ecclessiazusae* (Women in Congress). His libretto for C.S. Lewis' *The Lion, The Witch and The Wardrobe* had its world premiere in California and played in London and New York and is currently touring nationwide. For his play, *Theater Trip*, he was the recipient of a Thespie Award for Best New Play, and *Old Goat Song* won a drama critic's award in Los Angeles. His play, *The Spelling of Coynes*, has been included in *The Best American Short Plays* Anthology. His tragic piece, *The Balkan Women*, won the prestigious Barrymore Award for Best Play. His play *The Grand Christmas History of the Andy Landy Clan* was broadcast on 47 national public radio stations. Mr. Tasca received a grant from the Pennsylvania Council of the Arts to develop a new theatrical form, the Eurythmy, a system of movement to language, music and sound. Most recently, his tragedy, *Judah's Daughter*, received the Dorothy Silver International playwrighting award. The author is a member of New York's Dramatist Guild.

CHARACTERS:
Fanny Mae Spieler
Albert Spieler
Female Voice
Male Voice/Another Male Voice
Reverend Gerald Spieler
Jesus/Wild Man\Another Male Voice

Lights come up on FANNY MAE SPIELER, *a conservatively dressed woman. She addresses the audience.*

FANNY: I've come here today to the laboratory of my brother-in-law, Doctor Albert Spieler, in order to save my marriage.

[ALBERT SPIELER, *a man in a lab coat, appears.*]

This man, this tool of all that is evil in the world, has ruined my marriage by committing ...

ALBERT: At least let me tell my own side, Fanny Mae. Fanny Mae is married to my brother ...

FANNY: The Reverend Gerald Spieler ...

[GERALD, *immaculately groomed and polished in a three-piece suit, appears in another light.*]

ALBERT: Gerry ... my brother and I were brought up in the same home. We had the same upbringing.

FEMALE VOICE: [*Offstage.*] No more giggling in there, Albert! Gerry! It's 11 o'clock.

MALE VOICE: [*Offstage.*] One more report card from school like this and I'm gonna take my strap off!

FEMALE VOICE: [*Offstage.*] Who ate all the goddamned strudel your grandmother sent over?

MALE VOICE: [*Offstage.*] Put that dog out or I'll put you out!

FEMALE VOICE: [*Offstage.*] Who killed the roach with my *Ladies Home Journal*?!

MALE VOICE: [*Offstage.*] Get outta that bathroom! I'm late for work!

FEMALE VOICE: [*Offstage.*] I don't care if you do hate his guts. He's your brother, so shake hands!

ALBERT: You get the idea.

GERALD: It was a typical American family.

ALBERT: Gerry and I were both loved and beaten equally. The mystery is how Gerry grew up to be ...

GERALD: The Reverend Gerald Spieler, Jesus' four-star general here on earth ...

FANNY: An evangelist to all mankind.

ALBERT: And I, Albert Spieler, grew up to be ...

FANNY: A little liberal, atheistic, materialistic, anti-Christ, medical doctor!

ALBERT: It astounded me that I went off to college to become a scientist and Gerry ...

FANNY: Graduated with honors from the Midwest Theological Seminary in Nebraska.

ALBERT: Then he started a church ...

GERALD: And married adorable her, a minister's daughter.

FANNY: What a team we made. Gerald went on to become the leading Televangelist in America.

GERALD: "Jesus' General", our program was called.

FANNY: We were seen in all 50 states and were ready to go worldwide until ...

ALBERT: I began this special research. Why, I thought, do some people become so ensconced in religion, while in others, religion simply, as in the case of vaccination, does not take. Regardless of how bombarded I was with religious teaching — from Noah's ark to Lazarus' double dip at living — I could never regard religion as anything more than bunkum and scarum and hocum. But my brother ...

FANNY: Gerald actually spoke with Jesus!

GERALD: Oh, yes, I did! Often.

FANNY: Why, Gerald and Jesus were like Mutt and Jeff.

JESUS: [*Offstage.*] Gerald, this is Jesus.

GERALD: I'm all ears, Lord!

JESUS: [*Offstage.*] I have work for you, Boy, alot of work. I moved a little bit of heaven to the west coast, Gerald. I'm a producer now.

GERALD: Really, Lord?

JESUS: [*Offstage.*] Yes, Gerald. We are going on television! Buy a lot of expensive suits and get your teeth capped!

ALBERT: While Gerry took production meetings with Jesus, I studied over 100 families where some of the members of a family were religious, but had brothers or sisters who were not. *Ergo,* I postulated a theory that, since no environmental factors could account for religion taking in one sibling and not taking in another, there must be some biochemical entity in the brain stem that is different in the religious and the non-religious. It took years of dissection and investigatory surgery. I autopsied over 300 brains whose histories I could verify. I knew which brains were religious and which were not. What I found was this. [*He pulls down a medical chart of the brain.*]

FANNY: It is disgusting to show something like this in public!

[GERALD *crosses to* FANNY *and covers her eyes with his Bible.*]

ALBERT: There is a heretofore undiscovered gland the size of a pinhead under the hypothalamus here. In those who are bound by religion, it is visible to the human eye. In those who go to church on high holidays, or, say, only for funerals or a feel-good Christmas experience, it is visible with magnification. In the non-religious, the gland is almost non-existent.

FANNY: Who would believe this?!

GERALD: Yes. God is not a gland! [GERALD *pulls down a chart with a picture of Jesus on it.*] He is the Lord!

ALBERT: Everybody said … But I worked with several other leading brain surgeons who corroborated my findings. More years of study andresearch and I discovered a powerful drug that would shrink this Deus or God gland, as I did so call it. [*He holds up a small red pill.*] I call the drug …

GERALD: Deus-X.

FANNY: Oh, it's wrong. It is so wrong.

ALBERT: Deus-X is a substance that eliminates the small pin-head gland that makes one's emotions susceptible to religiosity. It impedes the bio-chemicals that make the gland thrive. With Deus-X, the gland just withers away and drops off. One dose. One hundred milligrams. That's all it takes.

GERALD: Moral castration!

FANNY: Gerald is so right. That's what it is, moral castration.

[ALBERT *releases the medical chart of the brain and it rolls up out of sight.*]

ALBERT: Fanny thinks I developed Deus-X because I hated what my brother Gerry became …

FANNY: Why was one of the first human tests done on a death row prisoner whom Gerald had brought back to Jesus?

[*A light comes up on* WILD MAN CODY *behind bars. He holds a Bible.*]

ALBERT: Wild Man Cody had killed his whole family of eight with knives and a gun, before the police captured him. Only his grandmother, Granny Lucy, was unscathed that day, because she was having a hip operation. When Wild Man Cody found out that he missed one member of his family …

WILD MAN: I escaped from jail, went to the hospital, and I strangled Granny Lucy in the intensive care unit. Then, my life's work done, I gave myself up.

FANNY: Gerald spent hundreds of hours praying with Mr. Cody ...

GERALD: Until ... poooof! Jesus flamed in his heart.

ALBERT: Ask any student of Hinduism: meditation changes body chemistry. The hundreds of hours of Bible preachment and contemplative prayer with Gerald had altered the Wild Man's brain chemistry in such a way as to actually — I saw it under his C.A.T. scan — inflame the Deus gland.

GERALD: Inflamed the love of Christ in his heart!

ALBERT: Head!

FANNY: Heart!

ALBERT: Head!

FANNY: Heart!

GERALD: Mr. Cody became born again and allowed Jesus to spin the wheel of his destiny.

FANNY: Mr. Cody said so freely.

ALBERT: Yes. The other death-row prisoners got so sick of listening to Wild Man that they all petitioned to have their execution dates pushed up.

WILD MAN: I am not afraid to die and neither should any of you others!

MALE VOICE: [*Offstage.*] Give it a rest, Cody!

WILD MAN: Jesus Christ waits for me on the other side of this vale of tears! The day I saw Jesus, I saw light! I saw life! I saw love!

ANOTHER MALE VOICE: [*Offstage.*] Somebody shut him up!

ANOTHER MALE VOICE: [*Offstage.*] This is cruel and unusual punishment!

WILD MAN: I love those I stabbed. I love those I shot. I love Granny Lucy who I choked. I love the police who arrested me. I love the warden here. I love the press reporters who wrote I should die.

MALE VOICE: [*Offstage.*] Warden, please, no more.

WILD MAN: I love the guards who sneer at me. I love my fellow death-row mates, even if you are pissed off at me for loving you so much. Oh, iron bars can't hold back my love!

ANOTHER MALE VOICE: [*Offstage.*] If I could get to Cody, I'd stick him, I swear it.

WILD MAN: Also, I love the executioner who will pop the lethal injection into my arm. I want to be executed. I really crave it. I do. You all know why? Because I want to repose with the Lord Jesus for eternity. I'm coming, Jesus! I'm coming! Won't be long!

ALBERT: In this same spirit of love, Wild Man Cody allowed me, under the prisoner medication testing program, to administer 100 milligrams of Deus-X to him.

WILD MAN: I love Doctor Spieler. I love his ass. Really, I do. Love, love, love.

GERALD: Fanny Mae and I, as Mr. Cody's spiritual advisors, had no objection.

FANNY: Sure. We believed the drug would do nothing to diminish the purification that Gerald had wrought.

ALBERT: But minutes after taking the dosage of Deus-X ...

WILD MAN: [*Standing and rattling his bars.*] I'm glad I killed my whole family! I hated them! They hated me! We hated each other! On Christmas morning, we *spat* on each other! The Codys were always honest! You know the thrill of seein' your loved ones gunned down? Huh? Killing Granny Lucy was best of all! She couldn't cook! Couldn't sew! And when you went near her, she stunk of goddamned old age! I hadda hold my friggin' breath when I strangled her! I hated her! I hate you! All of you! I hate the warden! I hate the guards! I hate the Bible! It takes up too much goddamned room in my cell! And I want my good behavior record torn up! You dumb bastards hear me?! Good behavior's for wimps! I want bad behavior records put in my file! You hear me?! I wanna be remembered with friggin' bad behavior written next to my name! You hear?!

[*Light goes out on* WILD MAN CODY.]

FANNY: Was it really the effect of Deus-X?

ALBERT: Yes. But one more illustration lest you think that Wild Man Cody was an anomalous fluke.

FANNY: At that time, Gerald and I still didn't believe in Deus-X.

GERALD: Nobody did. I even asked Jesus about the efficacy of Deus-X ...

JESUS: [*Offstage.*] Come on, Gerald. Huh. A pill. Your brother's playing head games with you.

GERALD: Mr. Cody, as far as Jesus, Fanny, and I were concerned, just went dotty.

FANNY: So when we heard about Miss Pringling ... Bertha Pringling never married. She devoted herself to prayer and good works for the poor. She was active in the anti-pornography crusade and marched down Main Street to protest against the public library for having the book, *Catcher in the Rye,* on its shelves. When the news about Deus-X and poor Mr. Cody came out in the papers, like Joan of Arc, Bertha Pringling ...

ALBERT: Called me a fraud. This apotheosis of puritanism challenged me to prove that Deus-X wasn't a hoax!

[*A light comes up on* BERTHA *with her back to the audience.*]

Bertha Pringling took the Deus-X pill in front of her minister and the entire Baptist congregation of her church. They all prayed and praised God for Bertha Pringling bringing to light the ostensible canard perpetrated by yours truly ...

FEMALE VOICE: [*Offstage.*] God bless you, Bertha Pringling!

ALBERT: [*As* BERTHA *slowly turns and lets down her severely pulled-back hairstyle and puts on make-up.*] Before the service concluded, Bertha gave her minister the finger, propositioned two elders, and sauntered out of the church, chucking the chins of the men on the aisle as she wiggled by. Now she has a job in keeping with her new world view.

GERALD: I prayed hard for Bertha Pringling. I did.

FANNY: But she's now a 900 telephone number sex fantasy girl for Fantasy Hot Line.

[*A red spotlight hits* BERTHA; *she produces a telephone. Belly dancing music comes up.*]

BERTHA: [*Exaggeratedly sexy.*] Lie back now and let me take you to a place where desire and reality ... merge ... into a paradise of pleasure ...

ALBERT: I was her first caller. Three dollars a minute. But I sort of owed her, you know...

BERTHA: Listen to the music, Albert, and watch me, in your erotic imagination, do the belly dance you requested ...

FANNY: Even Gerald called the 900 number, but just to verify that Bertha Pringling had, in fact, become a pig, and to give her Christian counseling ...

GERALD: Hello, Bertha?

BERTHA: I'm tall, Gerald, but I have supple limbs, swarthy almond skin. I'm made to titillate men's eyes ... See me ... See me dance ...

GERALD: Hello, Bertha?

FANNY: Gerald, are you calling that 900 number again?

BERTHA: My lips are red and pursed. My eyes have closed. My lids toned chalky blue with mystery. My hair, Gerald, is as black as the sin you are about to commit ...

GERALD: Alleluia! Praise the Lord!

FANNY: I had to have a 900 number block put on our telephone. Gerald was working too late.

GERALD: I always was a hard worker.

ALBERT: The results of Deus-X fascinated me. Fanny Mae and Gerry were disoriented by it. Fanny Mae began to lose sleep. Gerry found escape with the telephone down at his studio.

GERALD: Hello, Bertha?

BERTHA: Stay with me, Gerald. Watch my hips bounce ... my stomach move ... It's the body of an animal, Baby ... The rings on my ears and the ornaments on my nipples are bells ... Hear them ring ... the animal is decorated ... for you, Gerald ... My jet hair clings to the wet on the nape of my neck ... I'm moving faster now ... Barefoot in bells and bangles ... Right up close to you ... Reach out, Gerald ... touch the smooth, humid, throbbing stomach and ...

GERALD: Oh, God, yes!

FANNY: Stop!

[*The music stops.*]

That's enough!

[*The lights fade on* BERTHA.]

You see why I call Albert Spieler the anti-Christ? You see what he's done? You see?

ALBERT: It was science and religion head to head. And Fanny and Gerry were looking bad. While all the medical men and women in the world rushed to lionize me, religious groups, one after another, challenged me. Challenged Deus-X. I turned a whole seminary into circus performers. Large convents were left abandoned, habits strewn on the floors. Synagogues were converted into supermarkets. Muslims tried to kill me for transforming one of their holy men into a jockey ... I made the cover of *Newsweek* twice!

FANNY: It was sibling rivalry, that's all! You were trying to out-do a more famous brother.

ALBERT: Gerry?

FANNY: Gerald had planned to run for the Presidency of the United States, until ... until ...

ALBERT: One night on his T.V. program, when Gerry was half-crazed with belief in his powers to invoke the aid of the deity, my brother voiced before the whole nation ...

GERALD: I, through the the intercession of Jesus Christ will show, once and for all, that prayer with Christ is more powerful than any pill that the mere mind of an atheist could concoct.

[*Loud applause and music, as* GERALD *exits.*]

FANNY: I introduced Gerald that night. Ladies and Gentlemen, please welcome Jesus' General here on earth, The Reverend Gerald J. Spieler!

GERALD: [*Entering with his Bible to loud applause.*] Welcome! Welcome, Brothers and Sisters in Christ! Praise God! And welcome to the Lord's very own T.V. program. You all know why we're here tonight. I hold in my right hand the Book of Light, and in my left hand I hold 100 milligrams of the substance that my devil-driven brother calls Deus-X. Yes, it is the real thing. I asked him to come here tonight and place the pill in this hand, so he could not say we substituted an *M&M* for this ... this X ... Yes, X. Ex. Extinguish. Expunge. Extirpate. Exclude. All the "Ex's" that his kind would like to do with all that you and I hold sacred ... Well, this pill might've spooked some of those

others whose faith was weak, Brothers and Sisters. But Jesus'
General is made of Christian stuff!

[FANNY *leads applause.*]

Listen to me. Listen and watch all ye beloved of Him who produced us and this program ... as I promised, so I shall deliver.

[GERALD *pops the pill.* FANNY *leads more applause.*]

FANNY: That's what we think of the followers of Satan.

[*More applause and cheering.*]

GERALD: Thank you. I thank you. Jesus thanks you. He does. He's
telling me right now. General, he's saying, thank these people
for believing in me and not in the devil's little red pill. And as
I promised ... you see ... nothing. Absolutely nothing happened to me. Nothing! But I hold no hate for my brother and
neither should you.

[*He and* FANNY MAE *kneel.*]

Pray with us for my brother who sits in the control booth now,
but lives in the house of the anti-Christ. Please ... please pray
with me, Brethren. Later, I'll give you the 800 number, where
you can call in your donation ...

ALBERT: My brother, Gerry, had an unusually large and hard Deus
gland. To recoin an old phrase, he was hung like a televangelist ... The Deus pill took its time ...

GERALD: Dear Jesus, help my brother in trouble who has sought
to destroy you. Now that all the snares of Lucifer have failed,
help Albert Spieler see how he perverts the intelligence you gave
him to do ill against your name and ... and Jesus ... and ...
and ...

FANNY: What is it, Gerald?

GERALD: It just dawned on me, Fanny Mae ...

FANNY: Gerald ... Gerald, we're ... we're praying ... what just dawned? ...

GERALD: How ... how ... illogical — no, irrational that this all is ... praying ...

FANNY: Gerald! We're on the air!

GERALD: So what? Praying is illogical and irrational anytime ... It is in the same category as speaking to a chair or a shoe ... *Nobody ever answers a prayer! Ever!*

[FANNY *makes the "cut" sign to the control booth and begins pulling* GERALD *offstage.*]

Where're you pulling me? You that horny?!

[*He laughs. She struggles to get him off.*]

GERALD: You people out there should know that I screw around behind Fanny Mae's back any chance I get! A strange piece once in awhile, Brothers and Sisters, is a boon to a man's spirit. You want to be reborn again, do it with two women! Adultery is pure sport, that's all ... and for all you shut-ins, before the program is over, I'll give you a 900 number to call. Ask for Bertha Pringling. Hello, Bertha!

[*Two others enter from the wings and help* FANNY *pull* GERALD *off.*]

GERALD: Yanking me off?! Afraid if they hear the truth, you won't be able to bilk anymore money out of them?

]ALBERT: [*Releasing the picture of Jesus, which rolls back up.*] Don't look at me. He insisted on pitting the pill against prayer. I even tried to talk him out of it. I did.

FANNY: [*Re-entering.*] ... and that's why I came here today ... to save my marriage. After the incident on T.V., in front of millions, our whole audience changed ... Our program changed ... Now it's a talk show. Instead of "Jesus" General, it's called "General Mayhem". Gerald is the host and Bertha Pringling is the sidekick. Their guests are gays, transexuals, former convicts, authors, actors, in short, all the rot in the world ... and ... and ... and ... something ... something's going on between Gerald and that harlot, Pringling. I know it. Gerald'll come home and he'll ... he'll hardly look at me ... He tells me ...

GERALD: [*Sticking his head out from the wings.*] You're a prig and a prude! You're anti-life force! Get with it or get out, for Christ's sake! [*Off.*] Hello, Bertha!

ALBERT: Gerry wants Fanny Mae to loosen up. He wants her to dress up in a garter belt and stockings. He wants her to take her first taste of white wine. He wants her to start watching sexually explicit videos with him. In bed he wants her to perform ...

FANNY: I'm a minister's daughter! I can't do any of those things! They're sinful. They're vulgar. They're cheap. They're beneath me and I ... I ... I ...

[ALBERT *hands her a Deus-X pill and a glass of water.*]

But Gerald Spieler is my husband. He's all I had, and now I'm lonely ... so lonely that ... may God have mercy on my soul. [FANNY *takes the pill.*]

ALBERT: It didn't take too long before Deus-X shrank Fanny Mae's Deus gland.

[FANNY *undresses to colorful bra, panties, and garter belt.*]

Fanny Mae now administers to her husband's needs. She and Gerry and Bertha Pringling all live together in the same house. The three of them have never been happier ... They invite me for dinner and I often ... I often stay over and ... well ... let's leave it at that, shall we? My brother, Gerry, and I have become best friends. We enjoy good wine and conversation and ...

FANNY: We'll see you around eight, Albert?

ALBERT: [*As* FANNY *exits.*] You got it, Fanny Mae ... We're attending the Cody execution tonight. Witnesses. Search me. It's the kind of thing that turns Bertha Pringling on ...

[*Lights slowly fade.*]

I travel all over the world ... [*He holds up the red Deus-X pill.*] I leave it everywhere. As you exit tonight, there'll be a bowl of them in the lobby. Take one. They're free. Good night ... Good night and God leave you ...

Tom Topor

BOUNDARY COUNTY, IDAHO

Tom Topor

Tom Topor divides his time writing movies, plays and novels. His latest, a mini-series about the murder of JonBenét Ramsey, was broadcast by CBS in February 2000. His most recent movie, which he wrote and directed, was *Judgement*, with Jack Warden, Keith Carradine, Blythe Danner and David Straitharn. *Judgement*, originally shown on HBO, was based on the true story of a priest who molested his altar boys; it won a Writers' Guild of America award, was a finalist for a Humanitas Award and was nominated for several Emmies and Aces.

Topor is also known for his script of *The Accused*, starring Jodie Foster and Kelly McGillis. The picture won Ms. Foster her first Oscar as best actress and a Bar Association Gavel Award for Topor. His play, *Nuts*, which is still being staged all over the world, was produced on Broadway, and later adapted as a movie with Barbra Streisand and Richard Dreyfuss. The play won a Gavel Award and was nominated for two Tonys.

Topor's newest play, *Cheap*, a translation of Moliere's *The Miser*, was broadcast by National Public Radio, and had its world theatrical premiere at A Contemporary Theater, in Seattle, and is scheduled for production in Minneapolis, Oakland, Atlanta, London and Hong Kong.

The paperback version of his latest novel, *The Codicil*, was published recently by Hyperion. The hardcover edition of the book, a *New York Times* featured choice, has been translated into more than two dozen languages, including Japanese and Hebrew. In addition to *The Codicil*, he has published three novels. One of them, *Coda*, has been translated into eight languages and has become a cult favorite among both music and mystery fans.

Among the projects Topor is working on are the American feature version of the English mini-series, *Prime Suspect*; the film adaptation of Nelson DeMille's *Word of Honor*; an original screenplay about espionage, *Red Herring*; several anonymous production rewrites; and a new novel, *Defender of the Faith*.

Before he began writing at home full-time, Topor spent more than twenty years in the newspaper business, working for the *New York Daily News*, the *New York Times* and the *New York Post*.

It can all be on the record, I got nothing to hide. Turn on your machine right now. You need any help? You're way too pretty to be real good with mechanical stuff. Ready? Okay. First off, I want to say for the record that I'm not one of those guys who thinks there's a black chopper hovering around over my head. Second, I don't think the CIA planted a transmitter in my front tooth. Or my back tooth. Not that they don't — they just didn't with me. Look: all my own teeth.

I want you to get that down because it's really important for you to know — and I mean, you, you personally, and not just because you're a good-looking woman, but because you're the one here talking to me, and I believe in personal communication, one on one — I want you to know, I am not crazy. Not off the wall. Not nuts. Not paranoid even a little bit. I've got certain beliefs — Christ, you've got certain beliefs — and I hold those beliefs pretty strongly. Okay?

Now, what are these beliefs? Well, Christ. I believe in Christ. Freedom. I believe in freedom. Now, what if I tell you, we don't have freedom? I saw that expression. You're saying to yourself, oh, man, this is another Christian Identity wacko who's going to tell me how the income tax amendment was never ratified, or how he can't keep an H-bomb in his freezer. Uh uh. Freedom.

You ever hear of the Tuskeegee Experiment? You're an educated woman, you heard of that. That's where they gave all these Afro cons syphilis to see how many would die. You ever hear of the Oak Ridge Experiment? That's where they gave all these clerks and typists radiation, to see how much would kill them. Did anyone tell these people, hey, we're going to do stuff to you because you're no better than a goddamn dog, you're no better than a Jew at Auschwitz. No, nobody told them. Remember what they did to the Japanese. Into the camps you go, you little slant-eyed yellow traitors. And while you're in there, we'll just confiscate your homes, and your farms, and your grocery stores. Old history, right?

Look at these; these are not old history:

New York cops go on a rampage and shoot up a hotel in Washington. Who gets punished? Nobody. DEA raids the wrong house; infant has a seizure attack and dies. What happens? Nothing. Social Security makes a mistake, knocks 58,600 old people off the list; 245 starve to death. Who pays? Nobody. Assistant Commissioner leaves his girlfriend's body out with the trash. What happens to him? Nothing. Government auctions off 2,600 family farms in one month. Twenty-six hundred farms. Out! Go! No tickee, no washee. Where are those people — how many people is 2,600 families? Ten thousand? Fifteen thousand? My dad is one of them. Fifty-eight years on the farm. Out!

You ever hear of the Communications Assistance Enforcement Act? You missed that one, right? It orders every phone company in America to re-engineer their equipment so that every single phone in the United States can be tapped by the feds. You've got a phone at home, right? You've got a phone in your bag, right? By next year, every time you talk, the feds will be listening. I am not making this up.

My baby brother comes back from the Gulf, he's got a condition. Skin is falling off. Spots. Vomit. Fever. Pain. He goes to the VA. I've got a condition, he says, picked it up in Kuwait. Gulf War Syndrome, like Agent Orange in 'Nam. They give him a form; he fills it out, he sends it in. You want to see the answer? Here: Our research indicates — what a word, indicates; nice and slippery, indicates — that none of the chemicals or armaments or medications used by forces in the Persian Gulf exercise — exercise! — are the cause of any medical condition that has been brought to our attention. What language is that? Do you know? I don't know. Twenty years from now, you'll do a big story which'll prove that something happened to us in the Gulf just like Orange happened to the guys in 'Nam. Feds admit poisoning U.S. troops in Kuwait. Feds kill my baby brother.

Let's get down home. When you drove up here, you remember that sign you passed on your left? Government property, no trespassing. Big huge sign. Remember? Tell me this: how can the government have property and keep the people off it? We're the government, right. They're supposed to have our consent for everything. Consent of the governed.

You see what I'm getting at? There is no freedom because they never ask for our consent. We are not in charge. They are in charge, and I don't mean some they from outer space. I don't mean the goblins, or the aliens, or the trolls. I mean, the pols, the bankers, and the media, and the hired guns they buy. Now, they are not us, they are they, and they think different thoughts and they want different things than us. Okay. No problem. Live and let live. Cool. But they don't. The one thing they don't do is live and let live.

Look through the window, left. If you could see past those woods, you'd see Ruby Ridge. August '92, the feds go to Ruby Ridge to bust Randy Weaver; tax evasion. His kid Sam — he's 14 — comes out of the house and says to the Feds, what do you want? We want your ignorant, goddamn racist Nazi father. Bang. Sam is dead. Fourteen years old. Next day, Vicky Weaver is standing in the doorway of the house; she's got her baby girl at her breast. Actually, you look a little bit like Vicky Weaver, except you got curly hair. Who's that, one of the Feds says? The wife and kid, another one says. Fuck her, the first one says. Bang. Down goes Vicky Weaver. Dead. She lies there rotting for eight days while the Feds keep firing.

April '93, the Feds are in Waco, they're watching a cult? You know what a cult is? A cult is a religion without a politician in its pocket. The feds are bored, they're tired, they're pissed off 'cause four of their own bought it. Enough, the FBI says. Go in and take 'em out. Forty-eight grownups, twenty-four kids. Dead. The FBI guy who gave the orders, both times, he's promoted.

That's the they. Not just the ones who stop you on the road, or poison you on the battlefield, or steal your taxes, or lie to you in every paper and on every TV show, because they own every paper and TV show, not just them. The they is the ones who walk into your house and blow away your kids too.

Sorry. I get really twisted when I think about this shit. This stuff. Have you got kids? No, you don't look married. We've got kids. Boy and a girl.

You ever been at a birth? It's a hell of a thing, watching them come out. You put 'em there, and nine months later out they come. I didn't actually believe it with the first one. It was a hard connection to make. The nurse started to clean him, I say, no, give him to me, he's mine. I wipe him off. Did you know they're only about this big when they're born? I mean, tiny. Fragile. You got to hold it like it was a bird. Gentler even. Gentler, gentler.

[*Singing a few lines.*] 'I used to be cruel to my woman ...' etc.

I don't know why she left. Well, actually, I know why she left — I told her to get the hell out. She'd stopped being a wife. I don't mean that. I mean, a wife. One night, a bunch of us're talking about the Second Amendment, and Jed, my best friend, he's known us both since high school, he says, Beth, why don't you make a sampler of the Second Amendment. Friendly like. It's not an order, or anything — he can't give my wife orders. And Beth says, I don't do samplers. Like that. Like a knife. I don't do samplers. That's the beginning. A week later, it's, I don't do ... something, I don't know what. Just I don't do ... fill in the fucking blank. Sorry. Goddamnit, I miss her! No, I don't miss her, she had no right to leave. She knew I didn't mean it when I told her to get the fuck out. She had to know that. How could she not know that? We were together nine fucking years — how could she not know what I meant? She knew it! Goddamn stupid ugly cunt! Sorry.

The kids knew I didn't mean it. They tell the judge, daddy didn't mean it, if daddy has a drink, he shouts some, he breaks a couple of dishes, but he's not a bad daddy. He never hits us unless we're bad. They told the judge that, and I didn't coach them to, neither. They said it on their own. I swear on this Bible. I would not swear a false oath on the book of my Lord Jesus Christ. I am not a bad daddy. Ask my kids. Ask Jed. Ask Rick. Ask her goddamn sister. Ask anyone. I work, I provide, I spend time with the kids — hold on, hold on! That's what it's all about, it's right here in her affidavit, she tells the judge, hold on ... every minute he spends with the children, he fills them with hatred. Hatred! Do I look like the kind of man who'd fill my own kids with hatred? I don't do samplers!

Whoa. We are getting way off the track here. You don't need this stuff about Beth. That's not why you're here. You're here to find out about me, us, why we do what we do. Why the militia. Why the Christian Identity. Okay. Back to basics.

Now, I know if I start to tell you that there is a real conspiracy out there, and it started in a lot of weird religions before Our Lord Jesus Christ, and its whole purpose is to destroy Christianity and white civilization, and replace it with atheism and socialism and world government by the other races, by the black and the brown and the yellow races — that's the New World Order — you will tune out. You will go into blank space and let your tape recorder do your work. Fine. You don't have to believe me. You can pretend that the Gulf War was fought on your behalf, and the Vietnam War was fought on your behalf, and Iran-Contra was done on your behalf, and your leaders haven't lied to you, and cheated you, and murdered you for their own ends. You can live in the bubble. We don't live in the bubble. We live in the here and now. We are ready.

We are not going to let the New World Order take over. We know what the Washington-New York-Los Angeles Connection is. We know what Manhattan money power is. We know that Robert Rubin used to work for Goldman Sachs, and we know the people at Goldman Sachs break bread with Jesse Jackson. We know the people at Solomon Brothers talk to the people at Wertheimer and the people at Wertheimer talk to the people at Lehman and the people at Lehman talk to the people at Rothschild and the people at Rothschild talk to the people at Warburg Pincus, and the people at Warburg Pincus talk to Yitzhak Rabin. We know who owns America. We don't live in the bubble. We are ready. Doesn't mean we're violent.

I see you looking around and thinking to yourself, for somebody's who's not violent, this boy's got an awful lot of guns. You bet. And every single one of them legal. The Second Amendment to the Constitution gives me the right to bear these arms. You have the First Amendment, O.J. has the Sixth Amendment, drug dealers have the Fourth, Ollie North has the Fifth, the Afros have the 14th, and we have the Second.

This is an AK-47, it's legal. This is an AR-15, it's legal. This is a Glock, it's legal. This is a Smith & Wesson, it's legal. This is a SigSauer, it's legal. Cops like this piece. Here, hold it. Isn't this built beautiful? Here, here's a clip. Turn the piece over, slip the clip in, and hit it with the palm of your hand. All right! Hear that click? That is engineering. Now, put your left hand on top, on the slide, and pull it back, straight back. What just happened is a bullet come up from the clip into the chamber; now, let go of the slide, let go. Snap! Once you take off the safety, she's ready to fire. Your thumb is on the safety.

You want to shoot it? We can go outside if you like and you can shoot it; we got targets set up. One Robert Rubin, one Jesse Jackson, one Barbra Streisand. One Anita Hill. We like our little joke. You want to go outside? Okay, your choice. Better give it to me. Watch. I remove the clip, and — this is important — I jack the shell out of the chamber. Now, the piece is safe. Your forehead's a bit damp; you want something cold to drink? This didn't scare you, did it? Ah, I guess you're not used to guns.

How come? You live in New York, don't you? Plenty of guns there. All the Afros have them. Is Afros right? Or is it blacks this week? I know you can't say Negroes. You have a name for them, don't you — what is it, I heard it once ... schwarzes, isn't that it? Isn't that what Jews call Afros? That's cute, I like that. Maybe we'll use that in the next newsletter. And what do they call you? Hymies? Or is it Kikes? Yids? Me, I just say Jews. That's what you are, isn't it, just Jews? Did you know Christ was a Jew? Of course, he got smart. Kidding.

Can I ask you a personal question — is your hair really like that, or did you get a perm? Beth got perms. I said, why do you want to look like that? You look like a kike whore. My little joke.

What about you, do you do samplers? Kidding.

Let's go outside and shoot. Do you remember how I did this? Let me show you again. I turn the piece over, I slip in the clip, I hit the clip with the palm of my hand. Click.

It's quiet in here, isn't it? I can hear your breathing. Jesus, I think I can even hear your heart beating. Is that your heart? It's going pretty fast. Your forehead's damp again. Look at those patches under your arms. No offense, but I can smell your sweat. Are your legs crossed?

Where were we? Right: I put my left hand on the slide, I pull it straight back, I hear the bullet go into the chamber, I let go of the slide. Snap! I move my thumb to the safety. I'm ready to take the safety off. That's a pretty soft sound, it's not like jacking in a shell. You can hardly hear it. I'll bring the piece closer to your gorgeous Jew ear. Okay. I'm about ready to take off the safety. Are you listening? Listen.

Man, what if this is the last sound you ever hear? Listen. Hear it? The little tick. That was the safety going off. I'm ready. Are you ready?

Ha ha ha ha ha ha. Okay, let's go outside to the range. We'll take some pictures you can run with your article — militia man teaches Manhattan reporter how to fire a SigSauer. All I am is a teacher. That's all any of us is. We're good people. We're patriots. We believe in Christ and country. All we want to do is spread the word, and take back the United States of America. Got it? Great. Let's go shoot.

END OF PLAY

Cherie Vogelstein

ALL ABOUT AL

Cherie Vogelstein

Cherie Vogelstein has been produced numerous times Off-Broadway, Off-Off Broadway and across the country. Her one-act plays are a favorite among college students and have received over 60 campus productions. A recipient of the Hobson Scholarship for Dramatic Writing, The James Hammerstein Fellowship for Best Emerging Playwright of 1999 and a winner of the Jury Prize at the HBO Arts Festival. Cherie is currently published by Applause Theatre Books, Smith & Kraus, Ferrar Straus Giroux and Dramatists Play Service. Her current project *36 double D* is scheduled for a world premiere in the fall of 2001.

Cherie is also an astro-physicist.

CHARACTERS:
Gil, male
Lenny, male
Allison (Al), female

GIL, *very handsome and cool, sits with his back to us in an empty
coffee shop, reads the sports section.* LENNY, *downtrodden and
uncool, enters in raincoat and galoshes, furtively looks around, spots
GIL, quickly looks away, orders coffee. Nonchalantly,* LENNY *takes
cup and saunters by* GIL's *table. Suddenly, he stops, pretends to
notice* GIL *for first time.*

*Their initial conversation should be slightly awkward: the way it is
when casual friends meet after not speaking for awhile: full of sound
and excitement, signifying nothing.*

*The overhead clock reads 5:32. The figure in yellow slicker enters mid-
way through the action.*

LEONARD: Gil! [*Practically spills cup.*]

GIL: [*Looks up, friendly.*] Hey ... Lenny!

LENNY: What a surprise, what a coincidence!

GIL: Yehah — how ya doin', buddy?

LENNY: How are *you?* You look great!

GIL: Yeah? Well I'm doin' okay, you know, hangin' in there.
[*Awkward pause, then with some concern.*] ... how uh ... how are
YOU doin', Len?

LENNY: [*Jovially.*] Me? Well, I'm fine … alright, you know … not so good — [*Totally serious.*] — suicidal — I'm suicidal, Gil.

GIL: [*Sympathetic.*] Yeah, heard about you and Cindy. I'm sorry, man, we shoulda called.

LENNY: No, no *I* should've called you guys … it's just I've been so preoccupied, you know, with death, I haven't had any time. [*Cheery.*] So how's Allison?

GIL: Allison? She's real good … yeah, she should be comin' here —

LENNY: [*Excited.*] Really?!

GIL: Yeah.

LENNY: Here? Really? [GIL *nods.*] That's great, that is so great!

GIL: [*Puzzled by* LENNY's *enthusiasm.*] Yeah … any minute.

LENNY: [*Elated.*] I — I can't wait to see her, I mean what good luck … that is so fantastic, just terrific … incredible really …

GIL: [*Beat.*] You're not gettin' out much, are ya, Len?

LENNY: [*Instantly sad, sits, cradles his head.*] It's hopeless, Gil. I'm miserable, A WRECK: all alone during allergy season with my hair falling out and my gums big and bleeding — may I join you? —

GIL: [*Looks around uncomfortably.*] Uh —

LENNY: — I mean you don't know how lucky you are — wow — to have a woman like Allison, kind, darling, beautiful Al —

GIL: Len —

LENNY: [*Raptured.*] Oh God, God, I love her like a — [*Realizes.*] — a relative, a sister — [*Has to be honest.*] — a step-sister —

GIL: Yeah, I know —

LENNY: — but she's the last of her species, there are no Allisons left in this world — I thought Cindy might be an Allison, but she too turned into a Tina and I — [*He farts, looks up at* GIL *in shocked horror.*] — oh that is just inexcusable Gil — I don't know what to say —

GIL: It's alright — Lenny listen — [*They speak at the same time.*]

LENNY: — ever since Cindy left, my gastro-intestinal tract —

GIL: — I have to tell ya somethin' —

LENNY: — it has a mind of its own ... I oughta kill myself —

GIL: — when Allison gets here —

LENNY: — and I will — unless I find a woman —

GIL: — I think we're breakin' up.

LENNY: [*Shocked.*] What?

GIL: [*Beat.*] Yeah.

LENNY: [*Devastated beat.*] No.

GIL: [*Beat.*] Yeah …

LENNY: [*Beat.*] No.

GIL: Yeah.

LENNY: [*2 Beats.*] No.

GIL: [*Annoyed.*] LENNY!

LENNY: I'm sorry but I … can't believe it … I mean I just can't believe it — you and Allison, Allison and you … you're like Romeo and Juliet … Antony and Cleopatra … Lawrence Olivier and Danny Kaye —

GIL: [*With distaste.*] Oh man …

LENNY: I'm just so shocked — I'm in shock — wow — [*Shakes his head, louder.*] — wowza — [*Loud, smiling.*] — WOWZA!

GIL: Well listen … I'm just tellin' ya cuz maybe, you know, it's not such a good idea for you to be around when I tell her —

LENNY: Why, Gil? I'll be very quiet —

GIL: Right but uh … even though it's a cafe deal and I'm hopin' she'll keep the cryin' violent shit down to a minimum … I'll tell ya, Len, things might get pretty wacky — I mean, it's not easy breakin' a girl's heart … ya know?

LENNY: No … I don't know … I've dreamt about it …

GIL: Yeah well so anyway … I think that's what I'm gonna do. [*Pause.*]

LENNY: But can you just tell me, Gil, why? I mean ... why? Why?

GIL: What're ya askin' me?

LENNY: Well uh ... [*Beat, a tad perplexed.*] I guess I'm asking you why.

GIL: But now see, how can I answer somethin' like that? I mean ... there're about four million reasons and no reasons at all except some voice inside ya says it's gotta be done and you can't track down why. It's from a place of no logic it's not about logic it's bigger than logic. It's bigger than you. So you listen. [*Beat.*] Cuz once you stop listnin', once you stop, Lenny ... you're lost. You got no voices left.

LENNY: [*Beat.*] Are you shtupping someone else?

GIL: [*Immediate.*] Yeah.

LENNY: [*Horrified.*] Are you really?

GIL: [*Laughs.*] Hey gimmee a break, will ya? It's nothin' like that —

LENNY: So then what is it, Gil? Really. I want to know. I mean, I REALLY NEED to know! Everybody says they're looking for love, looking for love, looking for love, and what do they do the minute they get it? They flush it away — flush, flush, flush! [*Furious.*] This world is just one vast toilet of devotion, one big bathroom of romance where it's better coming out then it was going in — I'm sick of it I tell you, SICK! So listen to *this* voice, Gil, and listen good: You're not breaking up with Allison unless you have a damn good reason for it, a damn good reason! Do you hear me, Gil? Do you hear me? [*Yells.*] DO YOU HEAR ME?

GIL: [*Beat.*] Are you ... are you on some kind of medication, Leonard?

LENNY: [*Sits.*] Sinutab — I'm sorry, I'm sorry but [*Upset again.*] ... *you're* my friend too — [*Rises again.*] — I won't let you throw your life away! Sure, sure, I may know Allison longer but let's face it Gil — *we're* men — at least you are—and men have to look out for each other, care, bond, love — alright not love, love's too much but —

GIL: [*Genuine.*] Listen, I appreciate your concern, but uh you got your own problems, buddy —

LENNY: Please, I can always take on more — I welcome it! Gil, don't deprive me of a vicarious thrill, Gil, it's all I have left —

[GIL *is weakening.*]

— if I can help you two work it through, if we can talk it out —

GIL: Well, ya know, maybe that's not such a bad idea cuz like, she's probly gonna ask me why too, right? So maybe I oughtta prepare [*what I'm gonna say.*] —

LENNY: Yes, yes, you definitely should — wait — [*He turns away, ties napkin under his chin like a kerchief, turns to face* GIL, *speaks in falsetto.*] — now — hi, Gil, how are you?

[GIL *looks perplexed.*]

GIL: What're you doin'?

LENNY: [*In falsetto.*] I'm Allison —

GIL: Oh! [*Laughs.*] No offense, Len but you make a real ugly girl —

LENNY: [*Sticking to his role, falsetto.*] Did you want to speak to me about something?

GIL: O.K., O.K. yeah ... [*Serious.*] ... I did ... listen, Al, I haveta tell you something —

LENNY: [*Coquettishly.*] I love you, Gilly —

GIL: Yeah, I love you too. It's over. We have to break up.

LENNY: What?! Why?!

GIL: Why? [*Thinks.*] Honestly? Because ... I have a brain tumor —

LENNY: [*Falsetto*] Oh my God! You do?

GIL: No, no, no — seriously? We have to break up because ... I'm not good enough for you, Al, I think you deserve better —

LENNY: [*Falsetto.*] I do but I don't want better, I want you, YOU — [*Almost to himself.*] — moronic, greasy —

GIL: [*Oblivious.*] Yeah but the thing is ... I don't think I can measure up to this ... this IMAGE you havea me, ya know? I mean, sure we might be good today, we might be good tomorrow but ultimately, I don't have what it takes to fulfill a woman like you. And one day, one day I'm gonna look into your eyes and I'm gonna see — insteada the love — I'm gonna see somethin' else — I'm gonna see all the respect drained out and gone with only the hate left. And that's gonna break my heart, Al — [*Sobs.*] — it's gonna fuckin' break my Goddamn heart.

LENNY: [*As himself.*] Wow. Is that true?

GIL: No but it sounded good, right? [*Beat.*] I mean, you can't tell her the real shit, like ... like how you hate what she does in bed!

LENNY: What does she do in bed?

GIL: Oh, well, nothin', nothin', just ... ya know ...

LENNY: No I don't know — [*Casual.*] — I'm willing to know, I mean,
I'd pay to know —

GIL: Well it's no big deal really, just this thing she does sometimes
when ... when we're lyin' there ... ya know, after sex ... and I'll
be gettin' all comfortable, I'll be startin' to doze off cuz like ...
I'm FINISHED, right? — and allofa sudden, outta nowhere,
I'll feel this leg swingin' over on top of me, right over my body
while I'm tryin' to sleep —

LENNY: Is it *her* leg?

GIL: Of course it's her leg that's not the point — the point is while
I'm tryin' to sleep, I don't need some weight pinnin' me down
to the mattress, you know what I mean?

LENNY: Cindy bought a bunk bed when I moved in —

GIL: I mean, I'm not sayin' I don't appreciate Al's affection — I'm
not saying that at all — but there's a time and a place and after
sex ... I do NOT like to be touched, ya know?

LENNY: Cindy said even during, it should be kept to a minimum.

GIL: Yeah well Cindy was a pig —

LENNY: [*Defiantly.*] But she was my pig.

GIL: Listen, Len, can I just say? — she did you the biggest favor in
the world when she dumped you —

LENNY: I know, I know. That's the one favor women always want to do for me — [*With sudden emotion.*] — which is why I'm telling you it's lonely in New York, Gil — Allison is special —-

GIL: Yeah, I know she's special but ... but ... it's not just the leg thing, Lenny ... it's more than that ...

LENNY: You mean like a leg/arm kind of thing?

GIL: I mean like ... like — [*Thinks of something.*] — like the way she's so obsessed with her weight! I mean, all she ever does is ask me about it all the time: Like I won't have seen her for a day and I'll pick her up and first thing when she opens the door, she'll say, "Hi Gil do I look like I gained weight?"

LENNY: So?

GIL: So I'll say — No, Al, you look great — and she'll say — are you sure? — and I'll say — positive — and she'll say — no you're lying —and I'll say — why would I lie? — to make me feel good — no, no way — yes, I see it in your eyes — no, that's my contact lens Al, ya haven't gained an ounce since the day you were born — you promise? — I swear — you'd tell me if I did — of course — you promise you would tell me? — I promise — you promise you promise — I promise, I swear, I swear on my fucking life now give me a Goddamn stake to put through my head cuz I can't take it anymore, Lenny, it drives me fuckin' nuts!

LENNY: Why?

[GIL *rolls his eyes in frustration.*]

You mean because she's a little insecure about her figure ... needs a little reassurance, a little positive assessment of her weight?

GIL: Yeah but like ... why doesn't she just invest inna fuckin' scale? ya know what I mean? Why's it havta be such a big fuckin' mystery all the time?

LENNY: Gil, Gil, YOU'RE her scale, Gil, YOU —

[*Figure in slicker enters, sits bunched in corner.*]

GIL: But that's the thing — to me she looks great—so what's she so worried about?

LENNY: [*Shrugging.*] Maybe she's afraid if she got fat, you'd break up with her.

GIL: [*Softens.*] Well, yeah ... I would — but that doesn't mean she has to like "dwell," ya know? [*Guiltily.*] I mean, come on, Len — every guy wants his girlfriend to have a nice body, right?

LENNY: [*Nodding.*] Cindy gained 60 pounds while we were together.

GIL: God, I know — how'd you deal with that, man?

LENNY: I loved her for what was inside —

GIL: Deep, deep inside —

LENNY: [*Impassioned.*] Look, a good woman is hard to find —

GIL: *Cindy's* not hard to find — [*Spreads his arms wide.*]

LENNY: — Allison's not only beautiful inside AND out but she also —

GIL: Swallows.

LENNY: P-pardon?

GIL: Yeah but ya know, don't mention it, like when she comes.

LENNY: Listen, it's not an easy thing to weave into a conversation —

GIL: [*Thoughtful.*] The truth is, I don't really give her enough credit for bein' so … ya know, giving. I mean she's like a real tribute to her race — ahh, I shouldn't talk about this stuff, it's private shit. [*Beat.*]

LENNY: Gil, I understand if you don't care to share this topic with me but let me just say … I'd give my life to hear about it.

GIL: [*Hesitates.*] Well … alright, just between the two of us — [*Launches ahead.*] — what they say about Jewish girls is usually true, right? —

LENNY: Wha — what do they say about Jewish girls?

GIL: Ya know … that they're not too big on givin' head —

LENNY: Oh. I thought that was all girls —

GIL: — yeah well I'm just sayin', especially Jewish girls, so like to find a Jewish girl who not only enjoys goin' down, but is also willing to … imbibe—you're talkin' a rarity.

[LENNY *clears his throat, chokes a little.*]

Not to be, ya know, too crude —

LENNY: [*Quickly.*] That's alright, that's fine—

GIL: — but Al goes at it like a thirsty sailor on the hot Russian steppe and doesn't come up for air, ya know what I'm sayin'? — don't mention it, Len. Len?

LENNY: [*Nodding, choking, takes out inhaler.*] I'm just … I'm just having a little difficulty breathing. [*He uses inhaler.*]

GIL: [*Looks around, then at his watch.*] I wonder why Al's so late.

LENNY: Cindy was always late, Cindy —

GIL: Cindy, Cindy, will you forget fuckin' Cindy!

LENNY: It just ended last week, Gil.

GIL: Yeah well get over it already, alright? Get over it!

LENNY: [*Repeats to himself.*] Get over it.

GIL: I mean, the girl treated you like total shit!

LENNY: A little worse. [*Figure in slicker cries, they turn briefly.*]

GIL: Exactly! So just move on, ya know? Move on. You're free!

LENNY: Free.

GIL: Yeah, yeah — it's a guy's world, Len — I mean a 60 year old man can get a 20 year old girl — [*He snaps.*] — like that!

LENNY: Really? [*He snaps.*] Like that?

GIL: Nothin' to it.

LENNY: So that's it, that's my problem? I'm too young?!

GIL: No, no you're too nice! You like these girls who walk all over ya —

LENNY: I do, I'm grateful to them —

GIL: — when what you need is somebody nice, somebody sweet, a girl who gives ya support, makes ya feel good, really LIKES you —

LENNY: [*Like a kid at a toy store.*] They have that?

GIL: Yeah, yeah, ya just gotta give yourself a break, buddy, ya know what I mean? Ya gotta ... go for it, ya know? [*Beat.*] Just go for it! [*Pause.*]

LENNY: Gil?

GIL: Yeah, Len?

LENNY: When uh when Allison gets here ...

GIL: Yeah?

LENNY: When Allison gets here ...

GIL: Yes?

LENNY: When Allison gets here could I ... could I ...

GIL: [*Very calm.*] Finish the fuckin' sentence, Len.

LENNY: ... have her?

GIL: What?

LENNY: Well not "have her," "have her" is a silly expression but you know what I mean — could I ask her out — would you mind?

GIL: Would I mind? If you asked Allison out?

LENNY: Yes 'cuz you said —

GIL: You want to ask Allison out?

LENNY: Well ... yes.

GIL: [*Beat.*] *My* Allison, right? You mean Allison Kramer.

LENNY: Listen, if it's a problem —

GIL: No, it's no problem —

LENNY: — then I won't —

GIL: It's no problem just —

LENNY: Just what?

GIL: Just nothin', nothin' ... it's fine.

LENNY: Are you sure? Because —

GIL: Lenny. I said it's not a problem, okay?

LENNY: Okay. [*Beat, smiling broadly, happily.*] Thanks, Gilly.

GIL: Don't call me Gilly, alright? [*Beat, scowling.*] But I'm just thinkin' …

LENNY: [*Serious.*] Uh-huh, good, O.K. —

GIL: Ya know … what about "Cindy?"

LENNY: Oh. Well you said to forget her.

GIL: And that's it? That's all it takes — I say forget her and you're done?

LENNY: Well, Gil, I thought you gave me some very excellent advice and so I'm trying to follow up on it, is all —

GIL: Yeah, well, okay … good. [*Takes out cigarette, thinks awhile.*] But I haveta tell ya, Len, maybe this is sicka me an' all, but it kinda does bother me, ya know?

LENNY: [*Holds up coffee cup, happy and oblivious.*] This is not decaf.

GIL: [*Annoyed and confused.*] I mean you askin' Allison out! I mean cuz like … here you are, and and like … the body's still warm, ya know what I'm sayin'?

LENNY: Yes but in a way, isn't that better? [*Smiles broadly.*] I mean, that way she won't have time to mourn over the loss of you because I'll be right there to console her —

GIL: [*Getting angrier.*] Yeah but what I'm sayin' is I don't really want you there to console her —

LENNY: But ... Why, Gil? I mean, do you want to see her suffer?

GIL: Not at all. But I even more don't want to see her with you —

LENNY: But that's not very fair, is it? I mean, here you don't want her anymore —

GIL: I never said I didn't "WANT" her, Lenny —

LENNY: Well, you said you were breaking up —

GIL: I said I was thinkin' of breaking up — that the little, dancin' thought had walked my mind! But I mean I didn't realize that automatically gave YOU the green fuckin' light to pounce?

LENNY: [*Frantically looks towards door.*] But you said —

GIL: I said alotta things — because you asked me — as a FRIEND — what I was thinkin' so I — wait! Wait — is that what this whole gig has been about, Lenny, huh?

LENNY: Gig? What gig? Please, Gil, I'm gigless —

GIL: [*Rises, angry.*] All your concern for the what, why, why — were you just, ya know, circlin' the area till you could swoop down — like some little galosh-wearin' vulture —

LENNY: [*Backing away.*] That's not a very flattering characterization, Gil —

GIL: — and ... and what? just feast on my leftovers?!

LENNY: I'm kosher, Gil, please —

GIL: I mean, God! you are somethin', man — you are really somethin' —

LENNY: How can you say that? You know I'm not something —

GIL: — and ... and I mean for Allison, no less — Allison of all girls — don't you know how outta your league Allison is?

LENNY: Yes of course but — but you said to go for it!

GIL: It. IT. Not HER, you asshole!

LENNY: [*Summoning up his courage.*] But why not? [*Rises.*] Why not her?

GIL: Because ... because —

LENNY: [*Hitting his stride.*] Because what, Gil, HUH?! All my life I've watched the Leonards of this world lose the Allisons of this world to the Gils of this world and the Gils don't even care! They don't even fucking care!!! [*He throws saucer against wall.*] I'm sick of it, I tell you! I'm sick, sick, sick!

GIL: [*A little scared.*] Alright! You convinced me!

LENNY: It's men like you who destroy women for the rest of us — abusing and demeaning and rejecting them till they so totally lose their sense of selves they actually believe the REAL men are the men who treat them that way — !

GIL: [*Shrugs.*] Yeah ...

LENNY: — when in fact you're not real at all, you're just scared, scared of growing up, scared of yourself, scared that — just like you said in that speech — that one day you're gonna look into her eyes and see the hate because deep down you believe once Allison sees you, once she really sees Gilly for who he is, she'll see THERE'S NOTHING TO SEE!

GIL: Yeah? [*Rises.*] Well — [*Trying to find the right words.*] — fuck you, Lenny! Fuck you! [*Screams, grabs his collar.*] FUCK YOU! [*Silence,* GIL *lets go.*]

LENNY: I think I've offended you Gil — [*Sits.*] — I'm sorry —

GIL: No, don't be sorry, don't be sorry — who wants your sorry, Lenny? I mean, you think I think Al's just some lay ... some ... some pop? Well you're wrong. Allison's a GIFT, a PRIZE — who loves me! And so that's a VERY scary thing —

LENNY: [*Covers his face.*]

GIL: — I mean, it's alotta pressure — alotta — who wants to deal with dissappointin' a girl like that, ya know?! We're not talkin' some bitch whale beast like Cindy — we're talkin' Allison Kramer! And so even if a part athat — if part awhat you said — fear — whatever you said — even if it's something involved with that ... so what? I mean — what does that prove? That I'm no good, I'm shit? Because I'm — I'm human? That I may be scared of rejection deep down? Alright! So what, ya know? Deep down everybody's scared of rejection! Everybody!

LENNY: [*Puffing up his chest.*] I'm not!

GIL: Yeah? Well that's just cuz you're so fuckin' used to it —

LENNY: Damn straight! Damn straight I am! [*Rises, speaks quietly.*] Take a look at a real man, Gil — a man who's not afraid of rejection, of intimacy, of commitment, the dark — well okay I am a little afraid of the dark — but I'm not afraid of love! Love I embrace unguarded — and I love Allison! I want her, Gil!

GIL: [*Also rises.*] Yeah well so do I!

LENNY: [*Face to face.*] Yeah? Well ... well ... well step outside.

GIL: Why? [*Shakes his head.*] You wanna fight?

LENNY: No. [*Beat.*] I just want you to step outside — [AL *enters.*] — Al!

GIL: [*Whirls around to face her.*] AL!

AL: [*Coming over.*] Hi, hi — Lenny, what a surprise!

GIL: You're late —

AL: Oh I'm sorry —

LENNY: That's alright —

GIL: I was worried —

LENNY: So was I —

GIL: — cuz Lenny has to go —

AL: Oh no — do you really?

LENNY: No, not really   GIL: Yeah, he does [*Beat.*]
                          — you look great, Al —

ALLISON: [*Almost shyly, loves this.*] Do I? You don't think I gained a little weight?

GIL: No, baby — [*Meaningful beat.*] — and it wouldn't matter if you did.

[*They gaze into each other's eyes.*]

LENNY: [*Witnessing their passion.*] Actually, I really should be getting back ... you know, to my empty apartment ...

GIL: Here — [*Reaches.*] — let me hang up your coat — [*He helps her out of it, hugs her tenderly.*]

AL: [*Lovingly.*] Thanks, Gilly — [*Turns back to* LENNY.] — well Len, listen, we have to get together SOON —

LENNY: Yeah ... [*Sad.*] ... soon.

GIL: Soon. [*Loud and clear.*] We'll see ya, Lenny.

LENNY: Yeah. See ya.

[*He extends hand to* GIL, GIL *hesitates a second, then shakes, smiles.* LENNY *turns mournfully to* AL.]

Goodbye, Al.

[*He turns, walks towards door as* GIL *leaves to hang up coat. When* GIL *is out of sight,* LENNY *turns back, gives* AL *the O.K. sign, she smiles huge, signs it back to him. He smiles back, turns around, seems very sad, leaves. Black out.*]

THE END

The Scarlet Letter
by Nathaniel Hawthorne
Adapted for the stage by
James F. DeMaiolo

Leslie Fiedler pronounced it the first American tragedy. F.O. Mathiessen considered it the "Puritan Faust." Richard B. Sewall compared its inexorable dramatic force to King Lear. These chieftains of American literature were not, as one might suspect referring to a play by O'Neill. They are not in fact, referring to a play at all, but to a masterpiece of nineteenth century fiction. Until now, it appeared that Nathaniel Hawthorne's haunting drama of judgment, alienation and redemption would be forever confined to the page. The Scarlet Letter continues to be the most frequently read novel in American high schools today as well as one of the most widely circulated novels in the American library system. And now comes the stage version to do it justice.

A century and a half after its first incarnation, James DeMaiolo has forged an alliance of craft and spirit so potent in its own right and so faithful to Hawthorne's original that his stage version is certain to compel all non-believers to recant and take heed. The audience joins the chorus as they weigh the American contract of freedom against the fine print of convention and taboo.

Paper•ISBN 1-55783-243-9 • $6.95
Performance rights available from APPLAUSE

GHOST IN THE MACHINE

A New Play

by David Gilman

"A devilishly clever puzzler of a comedy...it traps us in a web of uncertainty till we begin to second guess with the characters."
—Jan Stewart, *New York Newsday*

"A vastly entertaining whodunit, a chess game with human pieces that does not limit itself...Gilman teases us with philosophical questions on the nature of reality..."
—Laurie Winer, *The Los Angeles Times*

"A tight theatrical puzzle, the play echoes both the menacing personal relationships at the center of Harold Pinter's work and the complex mathematical equations that animate Tom Stoppard...but it is also very much of its own thing."
—Hedy Weiss, *The Chicago Sun Times*

Ghost in the the Machine begins with a common situation-that of a missing fifty dollar bill-and spins it into intriguing questions of probability, chance and the complexities of musical composition: illusion and reality.

Paper•ISBN 1-55783-228-5• $6.95

BEST AMERICAN SHORT PLAYS 1991–1992

Edited by Howard Stein and Glenn Young

The Best American Short Play series includes a careful mixture of offerings from many prominent established playwrights, as well as up and coming younger playwrights. This collection of short plays truly celebrates the economy and style of the short play form. Doubtless, a must for any library!

Making Contact by **PATRICIA BOSWORTH** • Dreams of Home by **MIGDALIA CRUZ** • A Way with Words by **FRANK D. GILROY** • Prelude and Liebestod by **TERRENCE MCNALLY** • Success by **ARTHUR KOPIT** • The Devil and Billy Markham by **SHEL SILVERSTEIN** • The Last Yankee by **ARTHUR MILLER** • Snails by **SUZAN-LORI PARKS** • Extensions by **MURRAY SCHISGAL** • Tone Clusters by **JOYCE CAROL OATES** • You Can't Trust the Male by **RANDY NOOJIN** • Struck Dumb by **JEAN-CLAUDE VAN ITALLIE** and **JOSEPH CHAIKIN** • The Open Meeting by **A.R.GURNEY**

$12.95 • PAPER • ISBN: 1-55783-113-0 $25.95 • CLOTH• ISBN: 1-55783-112-2

BEST AMERICAN SHORT PLAYS 1990

Salaam, Huey Newton, Salaam by **ED BULLINS** • Naomi in the Living Room by **CHRISTOPHER DURANG** • The Man Who Climbed the Pecan Trees by **HORTON FOOTE** • Teeth by **TINA HOWE** • Sure Ting by **DAVID IVES** • Christmas Eve on Orchard Street by **ALLAN KNEE** • Akhmatova by **ROMULUS LINNEY** • Unprogrammed by **CAROL MACK** • The Cherry Orchard by **RICHARD NELSON** • Hidden in this Picture by **AARON SORKIN** • Boy Meets Girl by **WENDY WASSERSTEIN** • Abstinence by **LANFORD WILSON**

$24.95 CLOTH ISBN 1-55783-084-3 • $12.95 PAPER ISBN 1-55783-085-1

APPLAUSE

BEST AMERICAN SHORT PLAYS 1993-1994

"THE WORK IS FIRST RATE! IT IS EXCITING TO FIND THIS COLLECTION OF TRULY SHORT PLAYS BY TRULY ACCOMPLISHED PLAYWRIGHTS...IDEAL FOR SCHOOL READING AND WORKSHOP PRODUCTIONS:...' —KLIATT

Window of Opportunity by JOHN AUGUSTINE • Barry, Betty, and Bill by RENÉE TAYLOR/JOSEPH BOLOGNA • Come Down Burning by KIA CORTHRON • For Whom the Southern Belle Tolls by CHRISTOPHER DURANG • The Universal Language by DAVID IVES • The Midlife Crisis of Dionysus by GARRISON KEILLOR • The Magenta Shift by CAROL K. MACK • My Left Breast by SUSAN MILLER • The Interview by JOYCE CAROL OATES • Tall Tales from The Kentucky Cycle by ROBERT SCHENKKAN • Blue Stars by STUART SPENCER • An Act of Devotion by DEBORAH TANNEN • Zipless by ERNEST THOMPSON • Date With A Stranger by CHERIE VOGELSTEIN

$15.95 • PAPER • ISBN: 1-55783-199-8 • $29.95 • CLOTH• ISBN: 1-55783-200-5

BEST AMERICAN SHORT PLAYS 1992-1993

Little Red Riding Hood by BILLY ARONSON • Dreamers by SHEL SILVERSTEIN • Jolly by DAVID MAMET • Show by VICTOR BUMBALO • A Couple With a Cat by TONY CONNOR • Bondage by DAVID HENRY HWANG • The Drowning of Manhattan by JOHN FORD NOONAN • The Tack Room by RALPH ARZOOMIAN • The Cowboy, the Indian, and the Fervent Feminist by MURRAY SCHISGAL • The Sausage Eaters by STEPHEN STAROSTA • Night Baseball by GABRIEL TISSIAN • It's Our Town, Too by SUSAN MILLER • Watermelon Rinds by REGINA TAYLOR • Pitching to the Star by DONALD MARGULIES • The Valentine Fairy by ERNEST THOMPSON • Aryan Birth by ELIZABETH PAGE

$15.95 • Paper • ISBN 1-55783-166-1 • $29.95 • cloth • ISBN 1-55783-167-X

BEST AMERICAN SHORT PLAYS 1996-1997

Misreadings by NEENA BEEBER • The Rehearsal: A Fantasy by J. RUFUS CALEB • The Vacuum Cleaner by EDWARD de GRAZIA • Mrs. Sorken by CHRISTOPHER DURANG • Four Walls by GUS EDWARDS • I'm With Ya, Duke by HERB GARDNER • My Medea by SUSAN HANSELL • I Didn't Know You Could Cook by RICH ORLOFF • Tunnel of Love by JACQUELYN REINGOLD • Fifty Years Ago by MURRAY SCHISGAL • Your Everyday Ghost Story by LANFORD WILSON • Wildwood Park by DOUG WRIGHT

$15.95 • PAPER • ISBN: 1-55783-317-6 • $29.95 • CLOTH• ISBN: 1-55783-316-8

BEST AMERICAN SHORT PLAYS 1995-1996

Fitting Rooms by SUSAN CINOMAN • Scribe's Paradox or the Mechanical Rabbit by MICHAEL FEINGOLD • Home Section by JANUSZ GLOWACKI • Degas C'est Moi by DAVID IVES • The St. Valentine's Day Massacre by ALLAN KNEE • Old Blues by JONATHAN LEVY • Dearborn Heights by CASSANDRA MEDLEY • When It Comes Early by JOHN FORD NOONAN • American Dreamers by LAVONNE MUELLER • The Original Last Wish Baby by WILLIAM SEEBRING • The Mystery School by PAUL SELIG • The Sandalwood Box by MAC WELLMAN

$15.95 • Paper • ISBN 1-55783-255-2 • $29.95 • cloth • ISBN 1-55783-254-4

BEST AMERICAN SHORT PLAYS 1994-1995

A Stye of the Eye by CHRISTOPHER DURANG • Buck Simple by CRAIG FOLS • Two Mens'es Daughter by J.e. FRANKLIN • An Interview by DAVID MAMET • WASP by STEVE MARTIN • Hot Line by ELAINE MAY • Life Support by MAX MITCHELL • The Whole Shebang by RICH ORLOFF • Dear Kenneth Blake by JACQUELYN REINGOLD • The Cannibal Masque by RONALD RIBMAN • The Artist and the Model by MURRAY SCHISGAL • The Spelling of Coynes by JULES TASCA • The Wreck on the Five-Twenty-Five by THORNTON WILDER • Lot 13: The Bone Violin by DOUG WRIGHT

$15.95 • Paper • ISBN 1-55783-231-5 • $29.95 • cloth • ISBN 1-55783-232-3

APPLAUSE

BEST AMERICAN SHORT PLAYS
1997–1998
Edited by Glenn Young

This edition of Best American Short Plays includes a careful mixture of offerings from many prominent established playwrights, as well as up and coming younger playwrights. This collection of short plays truly celebrates the economy and style of the short play form. Doubtless, a must for any library!

Bellyfruit by **MARIA BERNHARD, SUSANNAH BLINKHOFF,** and **JANET BORRUS** • Little Airplanes of the Heart by **STEVE FEFFER** • The Most Massive Woman Wins by **MADELEINE GEORGE** • The White Guy by **STEPHEN HUNT** •Times Flies by **DAVID IVES** • The Confession of Many Strangers by **LAVONNE MUELLER** • Oedi by **RICH ORLOFF** • The Man Who Couldn't Stop Crying by **MURRAY SCHISGAL** • The Trio by **SHEL SILVERSTEIN**

ISBN: 1-55783-365-6 cloth
ISBN: 1-55783-366-1 paper